T0216359

Developing Bots with QnA Maker Service

Integration with Azure Bot Service and Microsoft Bot Framework

Kasam Shaikh

Apress®

Developing Bots with QnA Maker Service: Integration with Azure Bot Service and Microsoft Bot Framework

Kasam Shaikh
Mumbai, Maharashtra, India

ISBN-13 (pbk): 978-1-4842-4184-4
https://doi.org/10.1007/978-1-4842-4185-1

ISBN-13 (electronic): 978-1-4842-4185-1

Library of Congress Control Number: 2018964830

Copyright © 2019 by Kasam Shaikh

This work is subject to copyright. All rights are reserved by the Publisher, whether the whole or part of the material is concerned, specifically the rights of translation, reprinting, reuse of illustrations, recitation, broadcasting, reproduction on microfilms or in any other physical way, and transmission or information storage and retrieval, electronic adaptation, computer software, or by similar or dissimilar methodology now known or hereafter developed.

Trademarked names, logos, and images may appear in this book. Rather than use a trademark symbol with every occurrence of a trademarked name, logo, or image we use the names, logos, and images only in an editorial fashion and to the benefit of the trademark owner, with no intention of infringement of the trademark.

The use in this publication of trade names, trademarks, service marks, and similar terms, even if they are not identified as such, is not to be taken as an expression of opinion as to whether or not they are subject to proprietary rights.

While the advice and information in this book are believed to be true and accurate at the date of publication, neither the authors nor the editors nor the publisher can accept any legal responsibility for any errors or omissions that may be made. The publisher makes no warranty, express or implied, with respect to the material contained herein.

Managing Director, Apress Media LLC: Welmoed Spahr
Acquisitions Editor: Smriti Srivastava
Development Editor: Matthew Moodie
Coordinating Editor: Shrikant Vishwakarma

Cover designed by eStudioCalamar

Cover image designed by Freepik (www.freepik.com)

Distributed to the book trade worldwide by Springer Science+Business Media New York, 233 Spring Street, 6th Floor, New York, NY 10013. Phone 1-800-SPRINGER, fax (201) 348-4505, e-mail orders-ny@springer-sbm.com, or visit www.springeronline.com. Apress Media, LLC is a California LLC and the sole member (owner) is Springer Science + Business Media Finance Inc (SSBM Finance Inc). SSBM Finance Inc is a **Delaware** corporation.

For information on translations, please e-mail rights@apress.com, or visit http://www.apress.com/rights-permissions.

Apress titles may be purchased in bulk for academic, corporate, or promotional use. eBook versions and licenses are also available for most titles. For more information, reference our Print and eBook Bulk Sales web page at http://www.apress.com/bulk-sales.

Any source code or other supplementary material referenced by the author in this book is available to readers on GitHub via the book's product page, located at www.apress.com/978-1-4842-4184-4. For more detailed information, please visit http://www.apress.com/source-code.

Printed on acid-free paper

To my father, the late Mr. Ahmed Kasam Shaikh, who is always a source of inspiration for me, and to my mentor, Mr. Sabarinath Iyer.

Table of Contents

About the Author

Kasam Shaikh is a certified Azure architect, global AI speaker, technical blogger, and a C# Corner MVP. He has more than 10 years of experience in the IT industry and is a regular speaker at various events on Azure. He is also a founder of DearAzure.net. He leads the Azure INDIA (azINDIA) online community, the fastest growing online community for learning Microsoft Azure. He has a concrete technical background with good hands-on experience in Microsoft technologies. At DearAzure.net, he has been organizing free online webinars and live events for learning Microsoft Azure. He also gives sessions and speaks on developing bots with Microsoft Azure cognitive and QnA Maker service at international conferences, online communities, and local user groups. He owns a YouTube channel and shares his experiences on his website at https://www.kasamshaikh.com.

About the Technical Reviewer

 **Adwait Churi** is a certified Microsoft Azure Solution Architect and MuleSoft Certified Architect, a seasoned professional with 12+ years of experience (in the banking, financial service, and insurance fields), with LMS (Learning Management System), and in the healthcare and hospitality domains.

He is passionate about learning about technologies, including cloud, integration, micro-services, ETL, and DevOps. He has worked in various technologies, including Microsoft BizTalk Server, Microsoft Azure, MuleSoft, Microsoft Business Intelligence, and Microsoft SQL and has a range of experience in software application architecture and design, pre-sales, performance engineering, project management, and software development.

He also gives courses on Microsoft BizTalk Server, MuleSoft, and Microsoft Azure.

Acknowledgments

Very first, I would like to thank Almighty ALLAH, my mother, and especially my better half for motivating me throughout this process. I am highly thankful to Apress, for believing in me and considering me for this opportunity.

CHAPTER 1

Eagle-Eye View of Azure Cognitive Services

What are Azure Cognitive Services? What problems do they solve in the real world? These are a few of the questions that might come to mind when we come across the term Azure Cognitive Services. This chapter will dive in and find answers to these questions.

We are going to explore the QnAMaker service, which is part of Azure Cognitive Services, so it's a good idea to build the context around Azure Cognitive Services first.

Let's start by taking a look at what cognitive services are all about.

The What and Why of Cognitive Services

You must have come across terms like artificial intelligence (AI), machine learning (ML), and deep learning. These are part of intelligent conversations around the industrial word. Let's look at what these actually are.

© Kasam Shaikh 2019
K. Shaikh, *Developing Bots with QnA Maker Service*,
https://doi.org/10.1007/978-1-4842-4185-1_1

Artificial Intelligence

One of the simpler, smarter definitions of AI was quoted by the American computer scientist John McCarthy in 1956. He said that, "AI involves machines that can perform tasks that are characteristic of human intelligence."

This might not be the exact meaning of AI but is very close. For me, AI is about resembling human attributes like understanding, predicting, and acknowledging, which are no doubt complex tasks to emulate. There are different ways to achieve artificial intelligence, and one of them is by implementing artificial intelligence through machine learning.

Machine Learning

According to Arthur Samuel in 1959, machine learning is "...a field of computer science that gives computers the ability to learn without being explicitly programmed". So, it's about enabling your machine to learn without having to punch in hardcoded commands.

In as simple a way as possible, I will try to explain how machine learning works! Consider these phases:

- You have raw data with different patterns.

- The machine learning algorithm analyzes the patterns in the data. Techniques like deep learning are used.

- After analyzing the patterns, the algorithm creates a machine learning model, which is an output of the process.

- This model recognizes the patterns.

- The application seeds the data so that the models can recognize any patterns.

This is not an easy task to perform. It requires lots of data pertaining to different cases and expert training models. The second complex part is creating a machine learning algorithm and testing it with a certain number of real-world cases. This comes with no guarantee of successful end results. The task here is to expose your new model to the application. Now this exposure should not compromise security, availability, or performance. Another set of complexity comes into existence.

You need machine learning to make the application intelligent. For this, you need to have data, algorithms, and models in place. This is where Azure Cognitive Services help.

Azure Cognitive Services

Cognitive services are a set of REST APIs that expose the machine learning model to the outer world and help infuse smart, intelligent algorithms to hear, speak, recognize, and interpret user input into the applications, websites, and bots. Cognitive services are sometimes called MLaaS—Machine Learning as a Services.

Azure Cognitive Services reside in the Microsoft public cloud, which guarantees a secure, highly available and smooth performance. That's all we need in order to consume REST APIs in our application and leverage the machine learning capabilities with ease. A few cognitive services do need data to be uploaded by the users, but those services provide the appropriate algorithm.

Using Azure Cognitive Services will help you leverage machine learning capabilities in your application, with Microsoft expertise in cleaning and training the data, with no burden of developing complex machine learning algorithms. These all come ready from Microsoft. And you don't have to worry about availability, performance, or security.

Who Offers Cognitive Services

Cognitive services make implementing machine learning easy by consuming APIs and seeding data if necessary. Cognitive services are part of Azure and the Microsoft public cloud, and they are hosted at Azure data centers.

At the time of this writing, Microsoft offers 23+ cognitive services. A few are still in preview but are mature enough to use with applications. This count is growing rapidly.

Microsoft is not the only vendor that offers cognitive services. Others major vendors offering cognitive services include:

- IBM Watson

- Amazon Web Service

- Google Cloud Platform

They don't have as many services as Microsoft, but they too are growing. There are many others apart from ones listed here and they have their own expertise in offerings. But Microsoft is leading the way and includes all the benefits of using its Bing data.

Azure Cognitive Services APIs at a Glance

After having a brief look of why cognitive services are useful, let's dive into the Microsoft Cognitive Service offering. The objective here is to be aware of the offerings and understand what they do to help our applications be smarter.

Note   Microsoft Azure Cognitive Services are rapidly growing. The few services mentioned here could be renamed or removed or modified. I recommend you refer to Microsoft's official website for updated listings of their cognitive services.

Azure Cognitive Services are categorized in five different areas—Vision, Speech, Language, Knowledge, and Search.

I will explain at least one service and you can find out more using the provided links. It all comes with exposing REST APIs to consume and leverage the machine learning power in your applications.

Explaining all 23 services is not possible in one chapter. We also focus on the QnAMaker service offered by Microsoft Azure in coming chapters.

The objective here is to give you an overall view of the available services, so you understand how they can help you. Let's explore the services, one by one.

The Vision Category

As defined by Microsoft, the Vision category presents image-processing algorithms to smartly identify, caption, and moderate your pictures. As seen in Figure 1-1, at the time of writing this chapter, the following services are part of the Vision category.

```
https://azure.microsoft.com/en-in/services/cognitive-services/
computer-vision/
```

I provide a quick introduction to a few of them in a later part of this chapter.

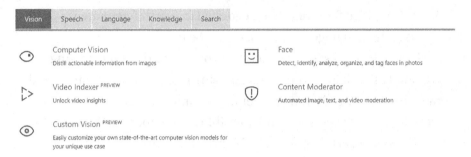

Figure 1-1. Services under the Vision category

Computer Vision

As described by Microsoft, Computer Vision enables you to extract rich information from images to categorize and process visual data and perform machine-assisted moderation of images to help curate your services.

Basically, it analyzes the image by type, color, etc. It provides lots of information about the image. It can tag the person's face and provide details like age and gender. It also gives score in percentages, for detecting images with adult content or racial issues. A score near to 1 means there's a high possibility that the presented feature is accurate.

This service is still growing and its accuracy is improving day by day. Let's look at an example. You can experience this service in action. Here you can select from a set of provided images or you can upload your own image or provide an image URL. To do this, visit `http://bit.ly/AzComputeVision`.

Figure 1-2 shows a sample image; let's go through the details it provides.

Figure 1-2. *The Computer Vision feature in action*

This random image has different options to select from. In Figure 1-3, notice that it has tagged my face as a person in the image.

Figure 1-3. *Computer Vision in action*

Figure 1-3 shows some more details about clip art type, line drawing type, color, and adult content.

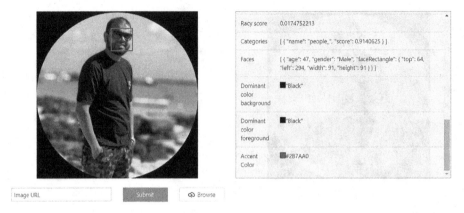

Figure 1-4. *Computer Vision identifies the people and colors in the image*

Figure 1-4 describes the person using the Faces attribute. It uses age, gender, and face coordinates and adds the background, foreground, and accent colors.

In some cases, these responses are not accurate and don't match the actual image. Let's see another image and then compare the differences in the response received. See Figure 1-5.

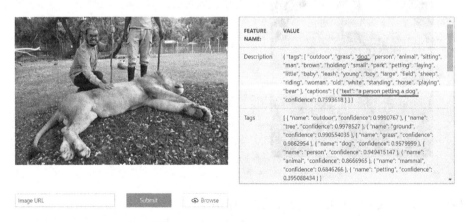

Figure 1-5. *Note the differences in the response*

In Figure 1-5, I am interacting with a lion, but the response analyzed it as a dog.

Figure 1-6. *Representing results of image*

Comparing Figures 1-4 and 1-6, you will notice under the Faces attribute, the my age differs. Figure 1-4 says 47, whereas Figure 1-6 says 40, although both pictures were taken on the same trip. Nether of these estimates is close to my real age, by the way.

The point here is that these services are still in their infancy and you can expect them to improve over time.

This service can be used in applications where users are allowed to upload images to the public domain. Analyzing and screening out images uploaded with any racial or adult content could save you lots of time in filtering out offensive images.

The Face Service

This service detects faces from a given image. It also compares two faces for similarities, along with identifying any specific face or person in a group of people. As a service response, it provides details to process facial images. It not only determines the human face coordinates, but also the emotion in the face. You can test this service at `http://bit.ly/AzFaceApi`.

This service can be used for authentication purposes, wherein users can be authenticated using his/her face images through facial coordinates.

The Video Indexer Service

This service unlocks insight data of any streaming video. From the speech, keywords, and sentiments, a person count can be achieved using this service. This service is still in preview. You can see it in action at `http://bit.ly/AzVideoIndexer`.

This service can be used to create video insights.

The Content Moderator Service

This service helps you moderate content in text, images, and videos. It helps you detect potential offensive and unwanted images, filter possible profanity, and find undesirable text, along with moderate adult and racy content in videos.

Try out this service at `http://bit.ly/AzContentModerator`. As mentioned, this service is best suited for content moderation.

The Custom Vision Service

Cognitive services are further subcategorized into predefined services and custom services. The major difference between the two is that a custom service uses your seed data and not Microsoft data. You can upload your own data and train it based on your use case and then use the same model for further actions.

The Custom Vision service is a custom service under the Vision category. At the time of writing this book, this service was in preview. Learn more about service at `http://bit.ly/AzCustomVision`.

Note   Microsoft Azure Cognitive Services are rapidly growing. The services listed here are presented by the Microsoft Azure Cognitive official web page. It's possible when you read this book, that there may be changes in the services listing with respect to their names and functionality. I recommend you refer to the Microsoft official website for updated listings under the Vision category.

The Speech Category

As defined by Microsoft, the Speech category converts spoken audio to text, uses voice for verification, or adds speaker recognition to your app. As seen in Figure 1-7, at the time of writing this chapter, these services are part of the speech category.

I provide a quick introduction to a few of them next.

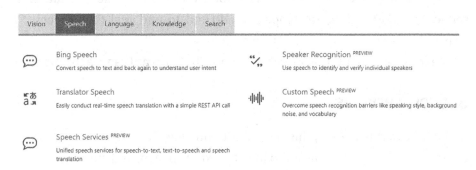

Figure 1-7. *Services under the Speech category*

Bing Speech

As per the definition stated by Microsoft, the Bing Speech service converts audio to text, understands the intent of text, and converts text back to speech for natural responsiveness. It works smoothly with multiple languages, such as French, German, and Chinese.

You can see this service in action at `http://bit.ly/AzBingSpeech`.

Speaker Recognition

At the time of this writing, this service is in preview. This service identifies individual speakers in the provided audio as input. You just record your voice to enroll and later use your voice as an intelligent authentication tool.

Also, this service is used to determine the identity of an unknown speaker. You input audio of the unknown speaker and it's matched against a group of selected speakers, and if it matches, it returns the speaker's identity.

The best use case for this service is to use it as a verification tool to verify the user's voice.

You can see this service in action at `http://bit.ly/AzSpeakerRecog`.

Translator Speech

The Translator Speech service API is a cloud-based automatic translation service. The API enables developers to add end-to-end, real-time speech translations to their applications or services.

Learn more about this service at `http://bit.ly/AzTranslatorSpeech`.

Speech Services

At the time of this writing, this service is in preview. It performs the complex task of converting audio to text, text to speech, and speech translation in a much simpler way.

It's best to use this when you're having conversation involving clients or customers who speak different languages. It uses a natural presentable voice.

Learn more about this service at `http://bit.ly/AzSpeechService`.

Custom Speech

This service is part of the Custom services subcategory as explained earlier in this chapter. This service at the time of this writing is in preview. Here you can have your own speech data train with unique requirements. In short you have total control over training the model, including your custom language and your custom models.

Learn more about this service at `http://bit.ly/AzCustomSpeech`.

The Language Category

As defined by Microsoft, the Language category allow your apps to process natural language with pre-built scripts, evaluate sentiment, and learn how to recognize what users want. As seen in Figure 1-8, at the time of writing this chapter, the following services are part of the Language category.

I provide a quick introduction to a few of these services next.

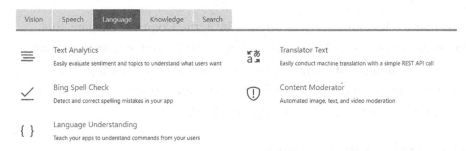

Figure 1-8. *Services under the Language category*

Text Analytics

This service performs major analyses of your text. It can detect the language of the text, detect sentiments, detect key phrases, and list any linked entities.

At the time of this writing, the process of listing linked entities is in preview. It helps you identify the linked entity in a phrase, for instance, the word "times," whether it stands for the "Times of India" or "Times Square".

This service is also part of the Azure Logic Apps as Action connectors. You can see this service in action at `http://bit.ly/AzTextAnalytics`.

Translator Text

As defined by Microsoft, the Translator API is a neural machine translation service that developers can easily integrate into their applications, websites, tools, or any solution requiring multi-language support, such as website localization, e-commerce, customer support, messaging applications, internal communication, and more. Developers can easily conduct real-time text translation with simple a REST API call. Learn more about this service at `http://bit.ly/AzTranslatorText`.

Bing Spell Check

One of the interesting services offering by Azure Cognitive Service, this helps users correct spelling errors, recognize the difference among brand names and slang, and recognize homophones as they're typing. It can be used as a spell or proof check in your application. You can see this service in action at `http://bit.ly/AzBingSpellCheck`.

Language Understanding

Language Understanding, or LUIS as described by Microsoft, is a machine learning-based service that builds natural language understanding into apps, bots, and IoT devices. It quickly creates enterprise-ready, custom models that continuously improve.

It's a custom service offering under the Language category. LUIS is an interesting service to work with, Azure Bot provides a separate template to integrate LUIS. It has its own web portal at `https://www.luis.ai/`.

You can see this service in action at `http://bit.ly/AzCogLUIS`.

The Knowledge Category

As defined by Microsoft, the Knowledge category maps complex information and data in order to solve tasks such as intelligent recommendations and semantic searches. As seen in Figure 1-9, at the time of writing this chapter, the following service is part of the Knowledge category.

Figure 1-9. *Services under the knowledge category*

QnAMaker

QnAMaker was announced as generally available at the May 2018 Build conference. It allows you to build an accessible database format, called a knowledgebase, for your existing FAQ content. It's the only cognitive service that comes with a Graphical User Interface to work on. You will learn more about this service in the coming chapters.

The Search Category

As stated by Microsoft, the Search category adds Bing search APIs to your apps and harnesses the ability to comb billions of web pages, images, videos, and news with a single API call. As seen in Figure 1-10, at the time of writing this chapter, these services are part of the Search category.

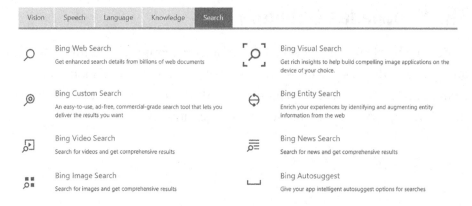

Figure 1-10. *Services under the Search category*

The services under the Search category widely deal with Search functionality. It can be a Web Search by Bing Web search, or a custom search by Bing Custom search, or a news or image search by Bing News Search and Bing Image Search, respectively.

Azure Cognitive Services offer a wide range of services under the Search category. Giving the app auto-suggest options or searching videos is now easy to plug in to your application with the help of these services.

Learn more about all these services at `http://bit.ly/AzSearch`.

Cognitive Services Labs

Cognitive Labs provides an early entry at the emerging cognitive services technologies for developers. These labs are not Azure services. Services in the lab are also being categorized in to Vision, Search, Language, and Knowledge categories.

At the time of this writing, considering all categories, there are 13 cognitive services. Figure 1-11 lists all the services under Cognitive Labs.

Cognitive Services Labs

Labs provides developers with an early look at emerging Cognitive Services technologies. Early adopters who do not need market-ready technology can discover, try and provide feedback on new Cognitive Services technologies before they are generally available. Labs are not Azure services.

Filter Labs [Filter by category ▼]

Project Gesture
VISION | EXPERIMENTAL ⊘

Incorporate gesture-based controls into your apps. Quickly define and implement customized hand gestures, creating a more natural user experience.

Learn more

Project Ink Analysis
VISION | EXPERIMENTAL ⊘

Cloud APIs to understand digital ink content created by users through document layout analysis and handwriting and shape recognition.

Learn more

Project Local Insights
SEARCH | EXPERIMENTAL ⊘

Score the attractiveness of a location, based on how many of a particular amenity are within a specific distance.

Subscribe

Project Event Tracking
SEARCH | EXPERIMENTAL ⊘

Find events associated with Wikipedia entities. Begin with a Wikipedia entity, and receive a list of related events organized by time.

Subscribe

Project Answer Search
SEARCH | EXPERIMENTAL ⊘

Enhance the user experience of your sites and applications by instantly answering search queries with relevant facts and results from across the web.

Subscribe

Project URL Preview
SEARCH | EXPERIMENTAL ⊘

Preview URLs to show users where they're going and help flag adult content.

Subscribe

Project Conversation Learner
LANGUAGE | EXPERIMENTAL ⊘

Teach new behaviors to task-oriented conversational interfaces through example interactions.

Learn more

Project Personality Chat
LANGUAGE | EXPERIMENTAL ⊘

Enhance your bot's conversational capabilities, by handling small talk, in line with a distinct chosen personality.

Learn more

Project Knowledge Exploration
KNOWLEDGE | EXPERIMENTAL ⊘

Enable interactive search experiences over structured data via natural language inputs.

Learn more

Project Academic Knowledge
KNOWLEDGE | EXPERIMENTAL ⊘

Tap into the wealth of academic content in the Microsoft Academic Graph.

Subscribe

Project Entity Linking
KNOWLEDGE | EXPERIMENTAL ⊘

Power your app's data links with named entity recognition and disambiguation.

Learn more

Project Anomaly Finder
KNOWLEDGE | EXPERIMENTAL ⊘

The Anomaly Finder API helps you to monitor data over time and detect anomalies with machine learning that adapts to your unique data by automatically applying a statistical model.

Subscribe

Project Custom Decision
KNOWLEDGE | EXPERIMENTAL ⊘

A cloud-based, contextual decision-making API that sharpens with experience.

Learn more

Figure 1-11. *Services under the Cognitive Labs category*

Looking at the list, we can say that Microsoft will be emerging stronger with interesting cognitive services in the future.

Explore the Cognitive Services Labs more at `http://bit.ly/AzCognitiveLabs`.

Pricing of Azure Cognitive Services

Azure Cognitive Services comes with no upfront cost, no termination fee, and most important, users pay only for what they use.

It has a free tier and a standard tier. This differs from the number of calls made to APIs called *transactions*. In addition to this tier, pricing could go up, based on the resources you use. For instance, Face APIs has pricing for Face Storage, whereas QnAMaker has pricing for Azure Search and Application Insights.

Developers can get their hands dirty working on Azure Cognitive Services, as all services come with the free tier.

Note   Microsoft keeps on updating its pricing options based on many factors. The pricing tier mentioned here could change in the future. Stay updated with the latest pricing details at `http://bit.ly/AzCognitivePricing`.

Using Azure Cognitive Services

Azure Cognitive Services are hosted in Azure datacenters. So, to use most of the Azure Cognitive Services, you need to have an Azure subscription to spin up the service.

You can have your own or use your organization's given Azure subscription to start with. The Azure free account is one of the best things offered by Microsoft Azure to hand shake with any Azure services. Azure Pass can also be used as one of the subscription options.

Note   To know more about how to create an Azure free account, I recommend you watch the videos and details available over the Internet. I recommend you look at this YouTube video: `http://bit.ly/AzureFreeAccount`. It explains the steps and advantages of having an Azure Free account.

Let's now dive into the Microsoft Azure Portal for creating Azure Cognitive Services.

GETTING STARTED WITH CREATING AZURE COGNITIVE SERVICES USING THE AZURE PORTAL

As a part of prerequisites for this exercise on how to get started with creating Azure Cognitive Service, you need a Microsoft Azure subscription.

1. Open the Microsoft Azure Portal, a web portal for creating and managing Azure resources. The Azure Portal link is at `http://www.portal.azure.com/`. Figure 1-12 shows the dashboard.

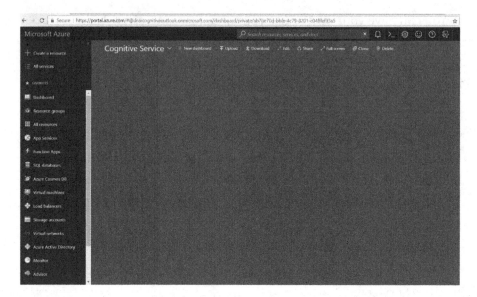

Figure 1-12. *View of the Microsoft Azure Portal dashboard*

2. There are two ways you can reach out to the Azure Cognitive
   Service registration blade. One way is to click on the + Create
   a Resource link in the top-left corner and then select from the
   different product categories. See Figure 1-13.

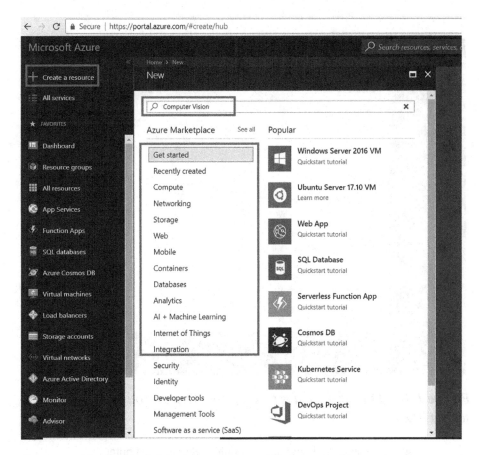

Figure 1-13. *One of the ways to open the Azure resource*

3.   Another way is to use the portal, which has a search box in the middle of screen, top bar. Enter the Azure resource name you are looking for, and it will list all the possible results, which will help you navigate to the resource. See Figure 1-14.

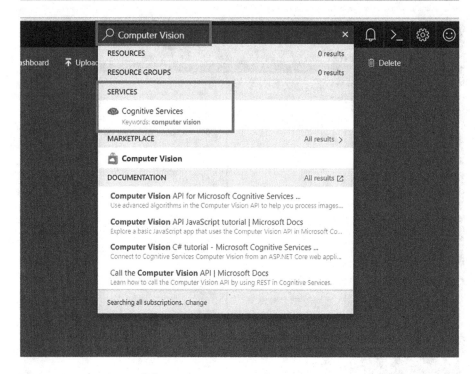

Figure 1-14. *One of the ways to open the Azure resource is by using a search box*

As you have seen in the Azure Cognitive Service Computer Vision area, we will create the same service as part of this exercise.

4. Click on + Create a Resource and enter the Azure Cognitive Service name into the search box, as shown in Figure 1-13.

This will show a page listing all the matching services, as shown in Figure 1-15.

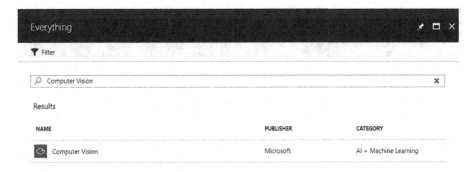

Figure 1-15. *Resulting services*

All the Azure Cognitive Services are grouped under the AI + Machine Learning product category.

5. Click on Computer Vision.

    This will present you with the blade explaining the service. Also, it comes with a button called Create.

6. Click on the Create button. See Figure 1-16.

Figure 1-16. *Service details with the Create button*

7. Clicking on the Create button will present you with the blade to create a service. You need to provide a few mandatory details:

- **Name**—Provide a meaningful name for the service for your reference.

- **Subscription**—Select at least one Azure subscription to proceed.

- **Location**—Specify the location wherein the service will be deployed once it's created.

- **Pricing Tier**—Select from options available as per your requirements.

- **Resource Group**—As this service is part of the Azure resource, it has to be organized into a logical grouping, a resource group. You can select any existing resource group or can create a new one.

This exercise will provide the details as follows (see Figure 1-17):

- Name: ApressCV

- Subscription: My Azure Subscription

- Location: West US

- Pricing Tier: F0 Free Tier

- Resource Group: Created a new resource group called Apress

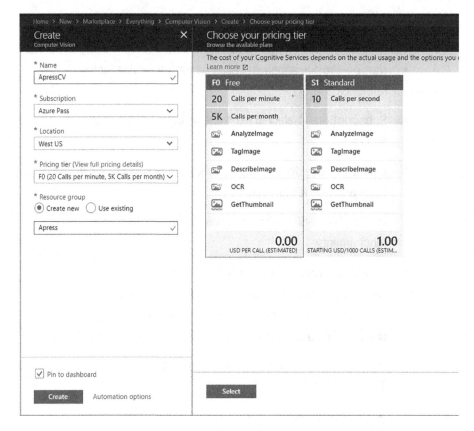

Figure 1-17.   Entering all the required details

8. After entering all the required details, check the box to pin the
    resource to the dashboard. Pinning helps give you easy access
    and tracks deployment status of the resource on the dashboard.
    This will look silly when you have very few resources, but it
    plays a very important role when you deal with multiple Azure
    resources.

9. Finally, click on the Create button.

This will start provisioning the service, which can be seen on the dashboard. See Figure 1-18.

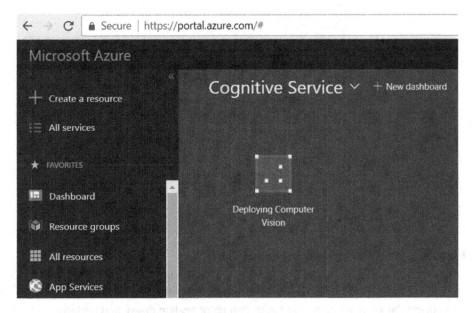

Figure 1-18. *Service being provisioned*

It will take a few minutes for the service to be deployed. Once it's done with deployment, a screen will be presented with the newly created Azure Cognitive Service. See Figure 1-19.

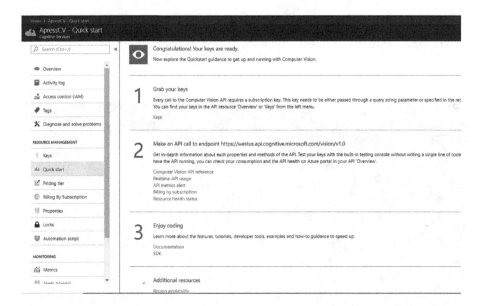

Figure 1-19. *Service created successfully*

You can now use the keys to make calls to the service from your application, manage the service pricing tier by scaling up or scaling down, and perform many other management activities. It also provides a Quick Start tutorial for a smooth start.

We explore the available managing section and its options more in the coming chapters, when working with the QnAMaker service.

Summary

In this chapter, we had a high-level overview of Azure Cognitive Services. You learned about the different Azure Cognitive Services available and how to get started with services using the Microsoft Azure Portal. Also, you learned a bit about Cognitive Services Labs.

In the next chapter, we will explore the Azure QnAMaker service. We will try to answer the what, when, why, and how about the QnAMaker service.

Before moving on to the next chapter, I recommend you explore Azure Cognitive Services over the Internet. Repeat the exercises detailed in this chapter on how to get started with Azure Cognitive Services.

Happy Learning!

CHAPTER 2

The What, When, Why, and How of the QnAMaker Service

In Chapter 1 you had a quick tour of what Azure Cognitive Services are all about and its offerings in the different categories depicting human characteristics, like vision, speech, etc. This chapter dives deeply into the Azure Cognitive offering called the QnAMaker service.

Note The QnAMaker service was announced as generally available in May 2018. It's continuously involving with respect to features, performance, and appearance. It's quite possible that you may find minor updates while experiencing live services, compared to what's mentioned in this chapter. I recommend you go through the current documentation before starting with the service implementation.

© Kasam Shaikh 2019
K. Shaikh, *Developing Bots with QnA Maker Service*,
https://doi.org/10.1007/978-1-4842-4185-1_2

Why You Need the QnAMaker Service

Before diving in to what the QnAMaker service is, let's look at the when and why.

Bots are the latest trend in the IT industry, whether it's a digital-driven company or a legacy-based enterprise organization. It helps us build communication with clients, product users, and services.

Communication plays a very important role in every organization, whether it's with clients, former clients, target product users, or employees. Communication plays a key role in conveying, justifying, selling, marketing, updating, and notifying all associated user verticals associated in an organization. Bots play a one-man role here to serve this purpose.

When it comes to bots, the objective is to be intelligent. Intelligence comes with the Microsoft Cognitive offerings, which infuse a human approach to create smart interactions. Let's consider a few real cases, where bots would be the right choice.

Say you are offering a product or service to end users, and you want all the users, including your existing customers and clients, to know more about these offerings. A large sales team could serve the purpose, but what if you have something in place to answer all possible queries with respect to the offering, without any human intervention? Yes, bots can do that!

Again, consider if your organization makes a few modifications to the conveyance claim policy or any HR-related policy. Apparently, every employee is keen to understand these small though tricky modifications and comes up with a certain number of queries with respect to the change. These queries are usually very common in nature. It's not always possible for the concerned team to respond to such queries all the time. An intelligent bot that's inexpensive to develop and maintain can play a key role.

There are thousands of such scenarios where we can implement bots to solve problems and make life easier. Now, this comes with a challenge of developing such bots. Not all employees are skilled to create bots with complex coding involved. Skilled employees come with huge salaries.

When you are creating a bot, it's like the bot is representing your organization or product to the outer world and to all key members associated with your organization.

Now, an organization must have a skilled developer with business domain knowledge, a business domain expert with development skills, or a consultant with development skills and domain expertise.

To overcome these requirements, Microsoft Azure Cognitive offers the QnAMaker service, a first of its kind with a GUI. A seasoned developer, business analyst, or even someone with no domain knowledge or no development skill can develop an intelligent bot using the QnAMaker service.

The best part is that these bots can be created in a matter of minutes, with RESTful endpoint enabling it to be compatible with any technology stack, such as Node.js, .NET, PHP, Python, and so on. Also, it can be integrated into any available bot frameworks.

It comes with many more interesting features and important compatibilities, for a professional from every sector to be well versed with.

Relax, as you will learn all about these supercool qualities in the coming chapters.

What Is QnAMaker?

There could be a whole other book on this topic, which is when to use bots! This section explains how the QnAMaker service can be the best choice when it comes to implementing bots.

QnAMaker is a cognitive service offering by Microsoft Azure, categorized under Knowledge AI. The QnAMaker service helps you power a service with question and answer capabilities from semi-structured or structured contents like FAQs, product manuals, etc., which are available in URLs, documents, and so on.

In simple words, the QnAMaker service extracts content from a given public URL or document and builds a concrete question and answer database known as a knowledgebase. It makes the knowledgebase available with a RESTful API endpoint to the outer world.

QnAMaker comes with an amazing graphical interface, one of a kind among other cognitive offerings. Have a look at Figure 2-1, which shows the QnAMaker Portal. It helps you create knowledgebases, manage the content extracted, train the data using different patterns of questions, and publish your service to the outer world. You can do this all without any developer experience and by writing no code.

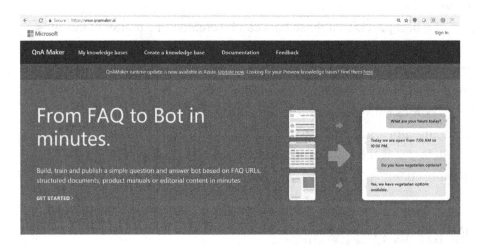

Figure 2-1. *The GUI Portal for the QnAMaker service (`http://www. qnamaker.ai/`)*

Figure 2-2 shows an overview of the QnAMaker process. Content in the form of FAQ public URLs and product manual documents are fed into the QnA Portal. QnAMaker extracts questions and answers from the provided source and forms a knowledgebase. This knowledgebase provides a RESTful endpoint, which then can be integrated into any bot frameworks or consumed by applications using different technology stacks. Also, it can be further integrated into different chat channels, like Skype, Facebook, Telegram, Web, etc.

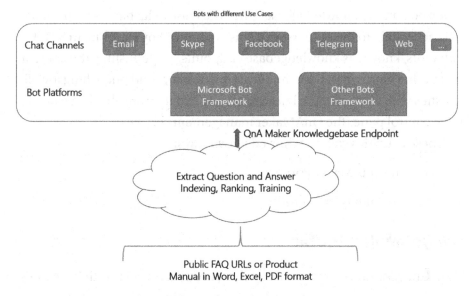

Figure 2-2. *Overview of the QnAMaker process*

The QnAMaker Architecture

The architecture was one of the major changes that happened in QnAMaker as GA. Now the architecture is built in Azure.

The QnAMaker stack consists of two major parts:

- The QnAMaker management services as a control plane

- The QnAMaker runtime as a data plane

The Control Plane

The control plane includes managing the question and answer content, which now will be referred to as the knowledgebase. When I say managing, that includes from creation of the knowledgebase to modifying it later. Being a cognitive service, it needs to be trained after every activity is performed on the knowledgebase. Once the knowledgebase is ready, it has to be accessible to the outer world. This is achieved by exposing RESTful endpoints, known as knowledgebase endpoints, by publishing the content.

In other words, creation, modification, training, and publishing are all activities with respect to the knowledgebase and they are all taken care of in the control pane (the QnAMaker management services).

These activities can be achieved in two ways:

- The QnAMaker Portal

- The management APIs

The QnAMaker Portal

One of the most amazing features of the QnAMaker service is that it comes with GUI interface. Hence, you can use it with minimal or zero developer experience. This widens the scope of users shaking hands with the QnAMaker service as a part of their application or requirement stack.

The QnAMaker Portal comes with a unique web URL, `http://www.qnamaker.ai/`. Refer back to Figure 2-1.

The Management APIs

These are a set of RESTful APIs provided by Microsoft, with a graphical interface and detailed documentation, for working with your knowledgebase.

You can use the APIs in .NET, Node.js, or any other application to deal with your knowledgebase. After being generally available, QnAMaker uses version V4.0. Refer to Figure 2-3, which shows all the APIs and their documentation.

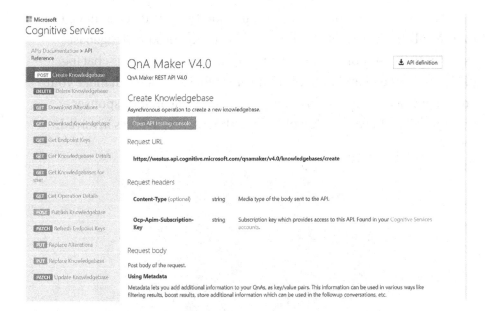

Figure 2-3. *QnAMaker V4.0 API documentation details*

Later, I show you how to create a knowledgebase using the QnAMaker Web Portal. Let's move on to learning about the data plane, i.e., the QnAMaker runtime component.

The Data Plane

When you create a knowledgebase, every single question and answer is stored in the Azure search, which is an AI powered cloud search service for web and mobile app development provided by Microsoft Azure. Every synonym and metadata related to your question bank is stored in Azure search.

The runtime is deployed to the Azure App service, a fully managed cloud platform as a service provided by Microsoft Azure, to easily develop, host, deploy, and scale your web and mobile application on the cloud.

Also, though optional, it adds Application Insights to its architecture, to store all chat logs being generated while using the knowledgebase as bot or to its endpoints through any given application. This chat log plays a vital role in updating your knowledgebase, which will make your knowledgebase more intelligent and more accurate in its responses.

Figure 2-4 shows the data plane and the Azure resources involved.

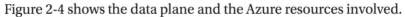
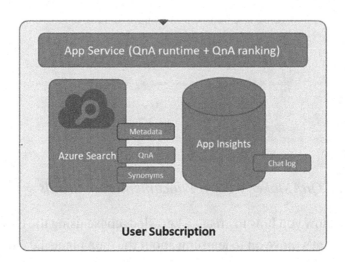

Figure 2-4. *View of the data plane, a stack in the QnAMaker architecture*

To summarize, QnAMaker has a reliable architecture built on Azure. All you need is the QnAMaker service and knowledgebase created, and this provides you with a RESTful endpoint to get connect to your application or to integrate with a bot framework.

For a better understanding of the QnAMaker architecture, refer to Figure 2-5.

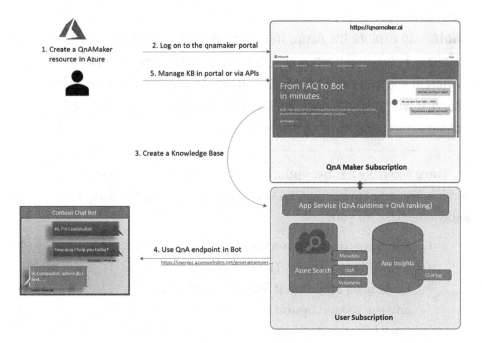

Figure 2-5. *Architecture of QnAMaker Service. Referred from the Microsoft website. (https://docs.microsoft.com/en-us/azure/ cognitive-services/QnAMaker/media/qnamaker-overview- learnabout/architecture.png)*

Creating a QnAMaker Service

Without going into more theory about this amazing service, let's get started with the important step of creating the QnAMaker service.

QnAMaker service, Azure search, Azure App service, and Application Insights are all part of Azure, and hence to use these resources, you must have your Azure subscription in place.

You can have a student account, an Azure free account, an Azure pass, or go a pay-as-you-go subscription. Get an Azure free account by visiting http://aka.ms/Free.

Note   To explore the Azure free account more, visit `http://bit.ly/az-free`. In the coming chapters, I provide you with a trick, wherein you can build your knowledgebase and use the QnAMaker service with minimal cost. For this book's exercise purpose, I am using Azure pass as my subscription.

Once you have a subscription, you can with creating a QnAMaker service. You need to have a QnAMaker service in order to create a knowledgebase for your bot.

1. You have two options to open a blade to create a QnAMaker service. The first option is from the QnAMaker Web Portal (`http://qnamaker.ai`) and the second option is from the Microsoft Azure Portal.

Note   For this exercise, I create the service from the Microsoft Azure Portal. We explore the QnAMaker Portal option while building the knowledgebase in a coming chapter.

---

2. Open a new Microsoft Azure Portal, `http://www.portal.azure.com`, and log in with your Azure subscription account email ID. Figure 2-6 shows the Microsoft Azure Portal with a custom dashboard created for this book.

Figure 2-6. *New Microsoft Azure Portal home page after logging in*

3. You can use the search box to search for the Azure
    resource you need. Just enter QnAMaker and
    it will list all relevant search results. Along with
    listing the path or link to create a new service, it
    will also list any existing services registered with
    your subscription. If you already have a QnAMaker
    service registered, it will list it in the search results.
    Also, it provides links for documentation related
    to services you are searching for. Many Azure
    developers skip using this search text box, but I
    recommend you use it for any Azure resource you
    are dealing with. Figure 2-7 displays the search
    results.

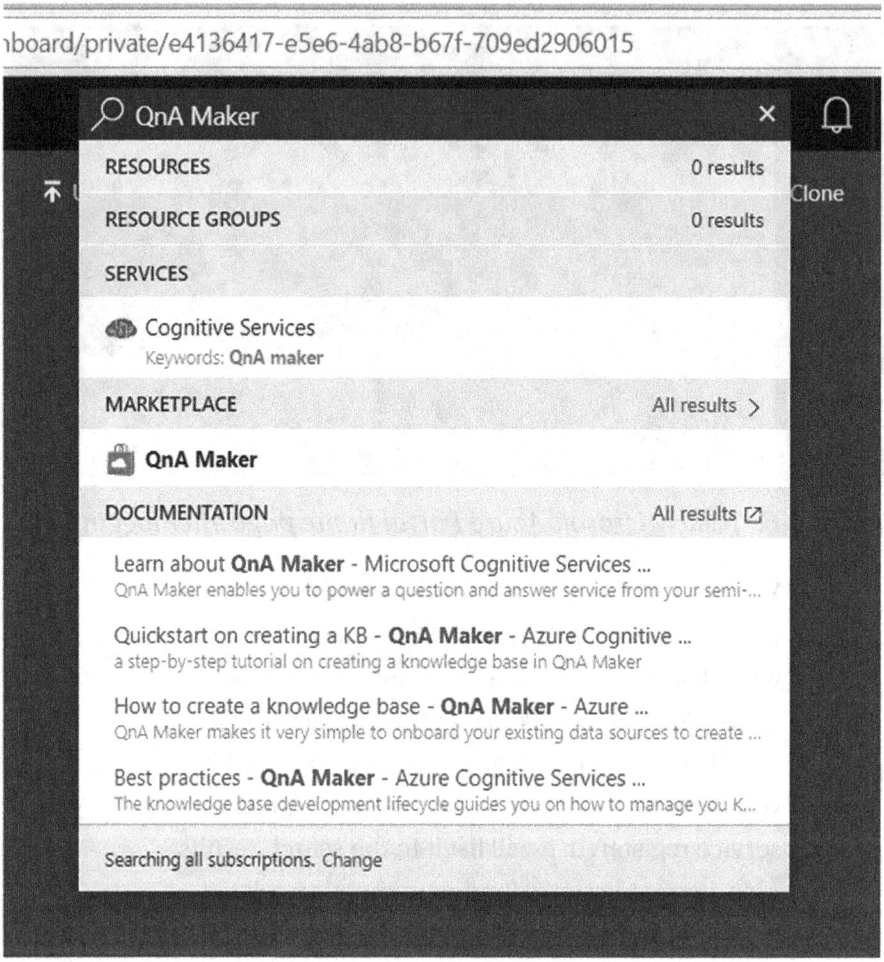

board/private/e4136417-e5e6-4ab8-b67f-709ed2906015

Figure 2-7. *Listing results via the search box in the Azure Portal*

4. Click on the desired option to proceed with registration.

5. Another way and the most used way of creating Azure resources is by clicking on the + Create a Resource link at the top-left corner of the Azure Portal's home screen. Figure 2-8 shows the link for creating an Azure resource.

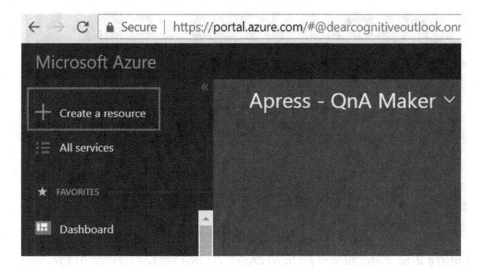

Figure 2-8. *The link to create an Azure resource using the Azure Portal*

6. Clicking on + Create a Resource will present you a wide range of products with services. As the QnAMaker service is an Azure cognitive offering, it falls under the AI + Machine Learning product category.

7. As shown in Figure 2-9, Navigate to AI + Machine Learning => Cognitive Services => QnAMaker Service.

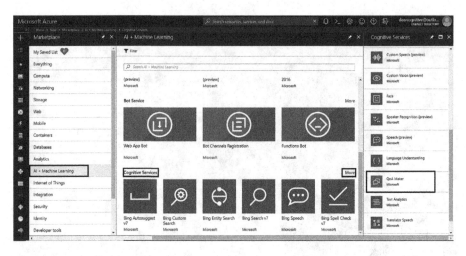

Figure 2-9. *Navigation path to create a QnAMaker service in the Azure Portal*

8. Also, when you click on the + Create a Resource link, along with listing products and related services, it also presents you with search box, wherein you can enter the resource name you need to create. It will list all related resources and details with respect to the resource name you entered. This is shown in Figure 2-10.

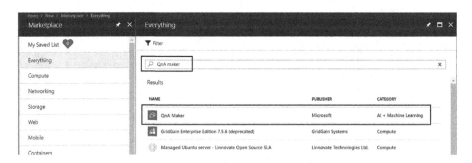

Figure 2-10. *The QnAMaker service in the Azure Portal*

You may be wondering why I am mentioning so many ways to create a resource. It's just that I want you to be more versed with using the Azure Portal, as the portal shares up to 70% to 75% of your service implementation.

9. Use any of these ways to reach the QnAMaker service, then click to proceed the registration. It will present you with a blade with a service description, including two buttons—Save for Later and Create.

10. Clicking on Save for Later provides you with easy access to the service. Means you don't have to navigate or search for the service, but you may have the service listed in your Saved list.

11. Click on the Create button to proceed.

Registering Your Service

Now that you've created your service, it's time to register it:

1. Once you click the Create button, the portal will present you with a blade where you need to enter a few details with respect to resource registration.

- **Name**—This will be the identifier for your QnAMaker service. It's mandatory to provide a name, and it should be unique. You can't have two QnAMaker services with same name in your subscription. Once you register and deploy it, the QnAMaker service will be listed by this given name, all over the portal, in the search results, in the billing information, etc. This is a reference name for your service. For this exercise, I used the name QnApress.

- **Subscription**—It's mandatory to have an Azure subscription to create a QnAMaker service. In this option, you will have a dropdown with all subscription listed associated with your account. You need to select a Azure subscription. Few developers have multiple subscriptions associated with the same account. If you have only one subscription, then that subscription name will be preselected. For this exercise, I selected my Azure subscription.

- **Management Pricing Tier**—An interesting pricing tier to select is QnAMaker's management pricing tier. Figure 2-11 shows the available pricing tiers. The decision with respect to the management tier is a very important factor.

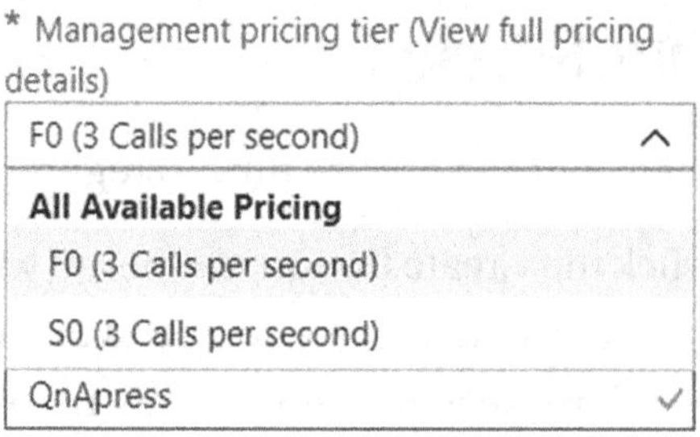

Figure 2-11. *Available management pricing tier options*

When you create a knowledgebase, you seed in it with FAQ URLs, documents, etc. This tier determines the count and size of the documents that can be used to build your knowledgebase. You will understand documents much better in the next chapter about creating your knowledgebase.

As shown in Figure 2-12, the management pricing tier comes with two pricing options.

- **F0 Free**—You can select the free tier only once in your subscription. You can't have two QnAMaker services using the free management tier in a single subscription. It allows you to make three calls per second to its associated knowledgebase. You can add up to three managed documents with max size of 1MB each.

- **S0 Standard**—The only difference with this tier is that you can add an unlimited number of documents with no limit on their size, although it has a few constraints with respect to the Azure search pricing tier. Again, you get to make three calls per second to its associated knowledgebase.

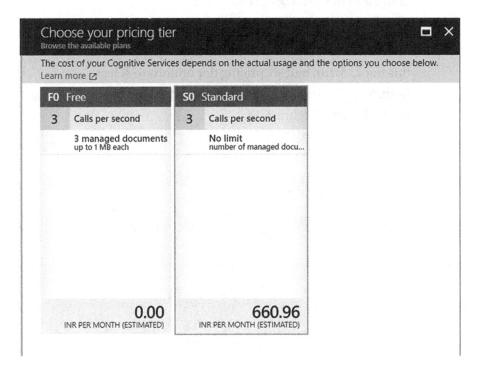

Figure 2-12. *Detailed view of the management pricing tier options*

2.   Click on the option you want to select and click on
     the Select button. You can later, after creating your
     QnAMaker service, switch between these tiers as per
     your requirements. For this exercise, I selected the
     free management tier.

3.   Resource Group: QnAMaker is a Azure resource,
     and it has to be in a logical grouping of Azure
     resources known as resource groups. All artifacts
     after QnAMaker service creation will be organized
     under the chosen resource group. You can select
     from existing resource groups associated with your
     subscription or you can create a new resource
     group. For this exercise, I created a new resource
     group and named it QnApress.

4.   Search Pricing Tier: This pricing tier is with respect
     to the Azure search service. At the time of writing
     this book, Azure had six pricing tier options to select
     from. Staring from free, basic, and standard, up to
     S3, as shown in Figure 2-13.

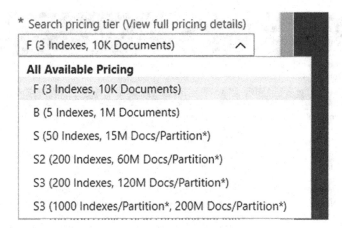

Figure 2-13. *Available Azure pricing tier options*

You can go with the free tier only once in your subscription.

5. Click on the View Full Pricing Details link for detailed information about the pricing options listed under the pricing tier search. Refer to Figure 2-14 for a detailed view of the pricing options available.

I highly recommend you explore the Azure Search service pricing options to understand and apply an accurate pricing tier. Visit `http://bit.ly/az-search-pricing` to learn more about the Azure Search service pricing details.

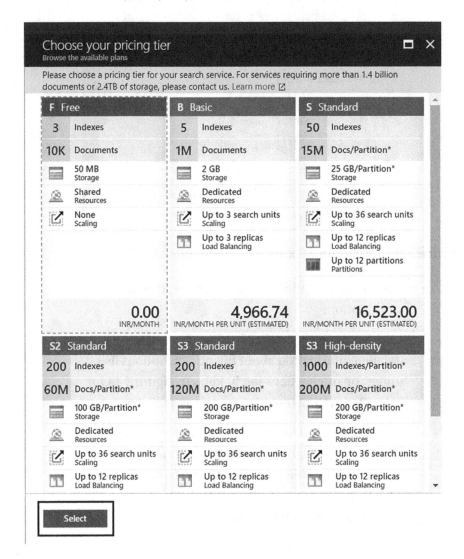

Figure 2-14. *Detailed view of Azure search pricing tier options*

6.   Click on the option you want to select and then click
on the Select button. You can later, after creating the
QnAMaker service, switch between these tiers as per
your requirements. For this exercise, I selected the
free search pricing tier.

7. Search Location: Here you can specify the location where you want the Azure search service to be deployed. It will list all regions where Azure search is available for deployment. Select the region you think your user traffic will be the busiest for much better performance. For this exercise, I selected East US for this option.

Figure 2-15 shows these fields.

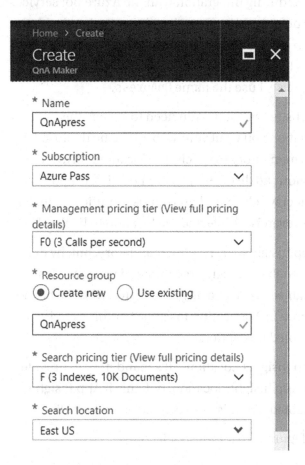

Figure 2-15. *Partial view of the QnAMaker service creation blade*

8. App Name—The next mandatory field is to provide the app name. As mentioned earlier in chapter, the runtime of QnAMaker is deployed in the Azure web app, so you need to provide a few details pertaining to the Azure web app. The name here should be globally unique. By default, it takes the same name as your service name. This name will be your knowledgebase service's hostname, and is later used during integration with the Azure Bot service. By default, the app service plan associated with the web app will be a Standard S1 tier. You can modify this later once the resource is created. For this exercise, I use the name QnApress.

9. Website Location—You need to specify the location you want your web app to be deployed. It's mandatory to specify the location. All available regions are listed in the Web Location dropdown. Select wisely, based on your user traffic region. For this exercise, I selected the location to be East US.

10. App Insights—This is not mandatory, but, by default, it's enabled. I highly recommend you have this enabled, as all chat logs associated with the bot are stored in Application Insights. For this exercise, I enabled this option.

11. App Insights Location—It's mandatory to provide an App Insights location, but only if App Insights is enabled. For this exercise, I selected East US.

Refer to Figure 2-16 for these selections.

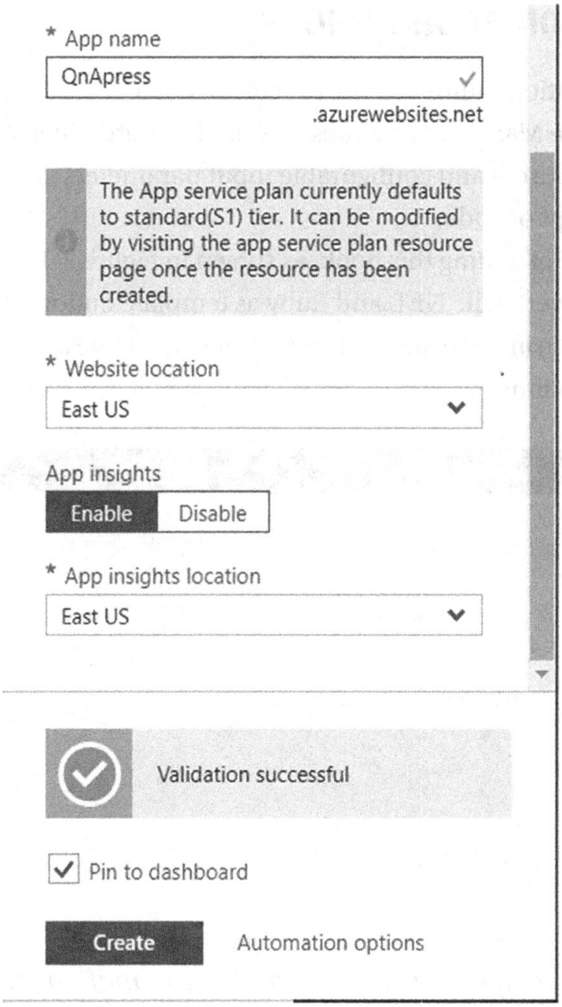

* App name

QnApress   ✓

.azurewebsites.net

The App service plan currently defaults
to standard(S1) tier. It can be modified
by visiting the app service plan resource
page once the resource has been
created.

* Website location

East US   ⌄

App insights

Enable   Disable

* App insights location

East US   ⌄

✓ Validation successful

☑ Pin to dashboard

Create   Automation options

Figure 2-16. *Partial view of the QnAMaker service creation blade*

Notice the link called Automation Options next to the Create button in
the bottom-right corner of Figure 2-16.

Using Automation Options

Automation options automate the process of deploying resources with the Azure Resource Manager templates in a single, coordinated operation. You can define resources and configurable input parameters and then deploy this with a script or code.

At the time of writing this book, as shown in Figure 2-17, Azure comes with a CLI, PowerShell, .NET, and Ruby as template options. We will not be using this in our exercise, but I wanted you to be aware of these automation options.

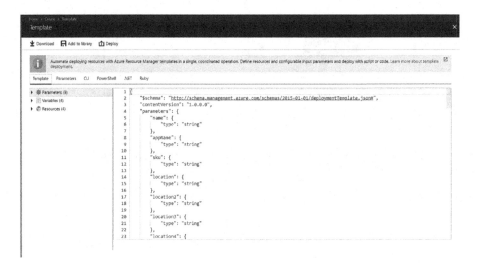

Figure 2-17. *Templates available for the Automation option in the Azure Portal*

Finishing the Project

Check on the Pin to Dashboard option is a good idea when you're using Azure resources. Using a customized dashboard with pinned resource will make managing resources much easier.

Finally, click on the Create button to proceed with QnAMaker service creation.

As shown in Figure 2-18, you can track the deployment status in your portal's dashboard, thanks to the Pin to Dashboard option.

Figure 2-18. *Ongoing deployment of QnAMaker service on the Azure Portal dashboard*

Finally, it will show up with the service name, status, and icon in the dashboard once the QnAMaker resource and all associated resources are created successfully. Refer to Figure 2-19.

Figure 2-19. *The QnAMaker service on the Azure Portal dashboard after successfully creating it*

Let's check the service creation under the resource group.

1. Navigate to the Azure Portal dashboard and find the Resource Groups link in the left pane. This link will present you with all the resource groups associated with your subscription.

2. Click on QnApress, which is the newly created resource group. Here you can see all the Azure resources being created, with the QnAMaker service creation along with its product type and location. The resources created should be the following:

   • QnAMaker Cognitive Service

   • App Service Plan

   • Web App

   • Application Insights

   • Azure search

If you find all of these services, this confirms successful
QnAMaker service creation.

Refer to Figure 2-20, which lists all the mentioned
resources under the resource group.

	NAME	TYPE	LOCATION	
	QnApress	Cognitive Services	West US	...
	QnApress	App Service plan	East US	...
	QnApress	App Service	East US	...
	QnApress-ai	Application Insights	East US	...
	qnapress-asur2metnz2x2kg	Search service	East US	...

Figure 2-20. *Resources created after successful creation of the*
QnAMaker service

3. Navigate to the QnAMaker service by choosing the
   QnAMaker service name from the list.

4. From the Overview tab, you can verify service details
   like the pricing tier, the endpoints it's pointing to,
   the location it's being deployed to, and its status. It
   also presents a link to delete the resource. This is all
   shown in Figure 2-21.

Figure 2-21. *The Azure Portal presenting the QnAMaker service*
Overview section

The service pane also provides a Quick Start option under the Resource Management section. This section is one of the coolest things to use when you're just starting using the service. All keys, documentation, and API references are part of this section. Refer to Figure 2-22 for a wider view of this section.

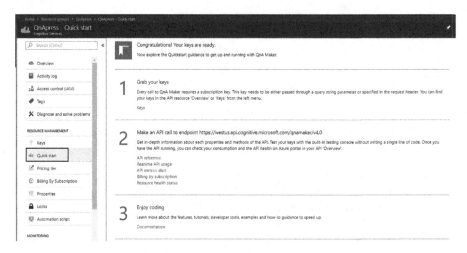

Figure 2-22. *The Azure Portal presenting the QnAMaker service Quick Start option under the Resource Management section*

Figure 2-23 shows the Keys section, which is also within the Resource Management section. These keys help authenticate the use of a QnAMaker service in an application. There is a primary key and a secondary key, and either one can be used. You can also regenerate both keys from this blade.

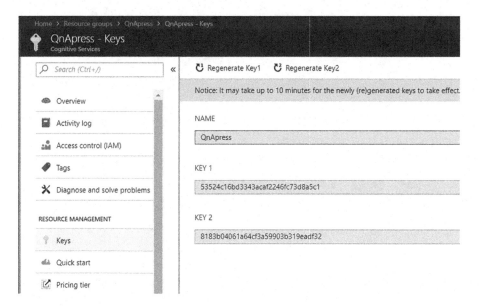

Figure 2-23. *The Azure Portal presenting the Keys option, under the Resource Management section*

Summary

This comes to the end of the chapter. You learned the whys and whens of the QnAMaker service. You also learned what the QnAMaker service is all about, and why it's the best choice in the market when it comes to using bots. You also started creating your bot, by creating a QnAMaker service using the amazing Microsoft Azure Portal.

In the next chapter, we develop a knowledgebase using the QnAMaker Web Portal and the newly created QnAMaker service.

Happy Learning!

CHAPTER 3

Creating the FAQ Bot Backend from Scratch

In the last chapter, you took a deep dive into the Azure cognitive offering QnA Maker service. We discussed what it is all about and why it's being used, and then you created a QnA Maker service using the Microsoft Azure Portal. In this chapter, you use this QnA Maker service to create a content backend for your bot or application, called the knowledgebase.

Knowledgebase   The knowledgebase is the content. It's a collection of extracted questions and answers, modified answers, manually added questions and answers, and metadata and synonyms. The knowledgebase is your FAQ Bot's backend; it's where the user will post a question as a request and it will send the matching answer if it's found as a response. In simpler terms, the knowledgebase is like the database for your bot. I will explain all these collection properties in more detail in this chapter.

© Kasam Shaikh 2019
K. Shaikh, *Developing Bots with QnA Maker Service,*
https://doi.org/10.1007/978-1-4842-4185-1_3

Ways to Create a Knowledgebase

You can create a knowledgebase using two different approaches. You can do it programmatically using the respective development stack IDE. For instance, if you want to create a knowledgebase using the .NET Framework and C# as the language, you need to use Visual Studio 2017. At the time of writing this book, it supported multiple programming languages, like C#, Go, Java, Node.js, and Python. In the future, there will likely be even more languages available for knowledgebase creation.

The second and quicker option is to create a knowledgebase by using the QnAMaker Web Portal. As I am presenting this book to a wide range of audiences and it's not specific only to developers, I focus more on the QnAMaker Web Portal for knowledgebase creation.

The Lifecycle of a Knowledgebase

Knowledgebase creation requires a few simple, but important, steps. The steps involved in creating a new knowledgebase are as follows:

1. Associate with the QnAMaker service.

2. Save and Train the knowledgebase.

3. Test the knowledgebase.

4. Publish the knowledgebase.

Let's explore the steps one by one, except for testing, which we'll cover in Chapter 4 in more depth.

Associating with the QnAMaker Service

To start:

1. Open the QnAMaker Web Portal at `http://www.qnqmaker.ai`.

   This page presents you with clean and clear links to proceed with the following steps:

   - My knowledgebases

   - Create a knowledgebase

   - Documentation

   - Feedback

2. As of now, the link of interest is the Create a Knowledgebase link. Click it to proceed.

   The next screen will present you with the five steps to follow:

   - Step 1: Create a QnA service in Microsoft Azure.

   - Step 2: Connect your QnA service to your KB.

   - Step 3: Name the knowledgebase.

   - Step 4: Seed the knowledgebase.

   - Step 5: Create the knowledgebase.

In terms of Steps 1 and 2, either one is mandatory in order to proceed with the next steps. Steps 3 and 5 are also mandatory, while Step 4 is optional. This information is just to give you a heads up, and I will explain each step in detail in the following sections.

Step 1: Create a QnA Service in Microsoft Azure

When I first explained the QnA Maker architecture, I mentioned its runtime stack. Its content is deployed to the Azure search. When you're creating a knowledgebase, you must associated it with a QnA Maker service. So, once the knowledgebase is created, its content has to be deployed to the Azure search.

Step 1 shows a button that enables you to create a QnA Maker service. Clicking on this button will navigate you to the Microsoft Azure Portal and open the QnA Maker Service blade, as shown in Figure 3-1. If you want to, you can create a new QnA Maker service. Or, if you already have QnA Maker service, you can directly associate your knowledgebase with the existing QnA Maker service.

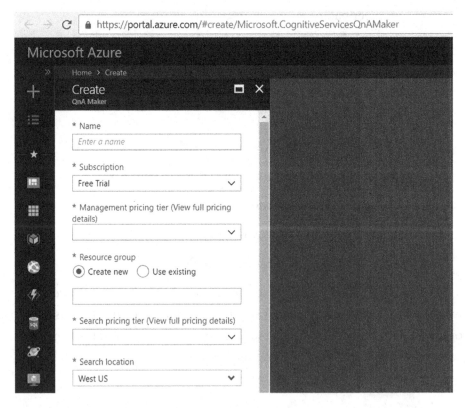

Figure 3-1. *Presenting the QnA Service Creation blade from the Azure Portal*

Step 2: Associate an Existing QnA Maker Service with a Knowledgebase

Step 2 of the QnA Maker Web Portal process enables us to associate an existing QnA Maker service with the newly created knowledgebase. Hence, as I mentioned earlier, one of the Steps 1 and 2 are mandatory. In the last chapter, you saw how to create an QnA Maker service using the Microsoft Azure Portal. I will use that same service here to perform Step 2.

As seen in Figure 3-2, Step 2 presents three dropdowns to select from:

- **Microsoft Azure Directory ID**—This is the username or ID you use to connect to the Microsoft Azure Portal and the QnA Maker Web Portal.

- **Azure subscription name**—Once you select an ID from the first dropdown, all the Azure subscriptions associated with that ID will be listed. Select the subscription you want to proceed with.

- **Azure QnA service**—After selecting the Azure subscription, the QnA Maker service created under the respective subscription is listed. Select the QnA Maker service you want your knowledgebase to be associated with.

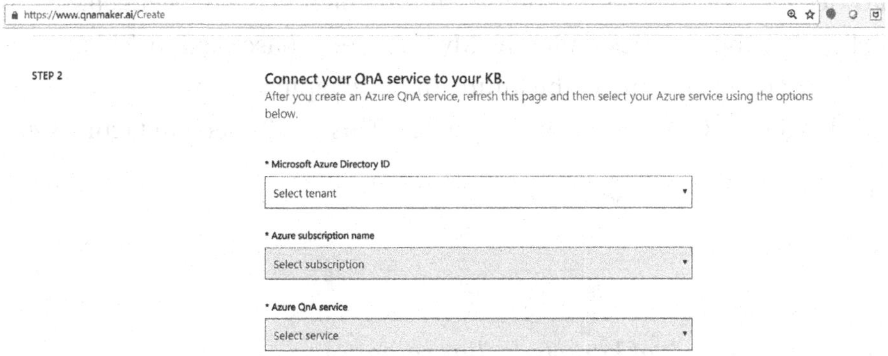

Figure 3-2. Step 2 of knowledgebase creation

Figure 3-3 shows the selected option I am going to use in this chapter. I selected my username or ID, my Azure subscription, and the QnA Maker service created in the earlier chapter. The knowledgebase I will be creating in this chapter will now be associated with the QnA Maker service called QnApress.

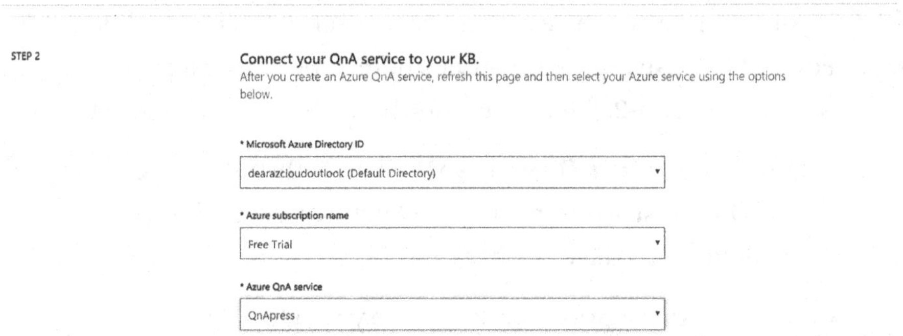

STEP 2

Connect your QnA service to your KB.
After you create an Azure QnA service, refresh this page and then select your Azure service using the options below.

* Microsoft Azure Directory ID

dearazcloudoutlook (Default Directory)

* Azure subscription name

Free Trial

* Azure QnA service

QnApress

Figure 3-3. *Step 2 of knowledgebase creation after selecting the appropriate values*

Step 3: Name the Knowledgebase Service

Once you're done creating the QnA Maker service and associating your knowledgebase with the service, Step 3 is about naming the knowledgebase service. It's mandatory to provide a name for your knowledgebase. This name is only for future reference. Knowledgebases are listed by their names under the My Knowledgebase section. This can be changed anytime in the future. In this chapter, I name the knowledgebase QnApress Knowledgebase. This can be seen in Figure 3-4.

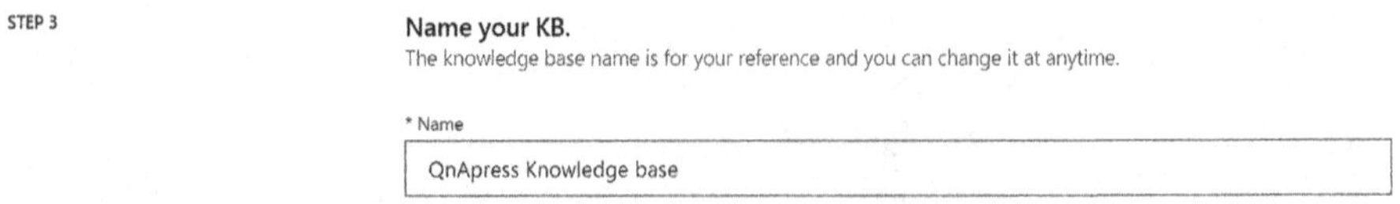

STEP 3

Name your KB.
The knowledge base name is for your reference and you can change it at anytime.

* Name

QnApress Knowledge base

Figure 3-4. *Step 3 of knowledgebase creation*

Step 4: Provide the Content Source

Moving to Step 4. Although it's not mandatory at this time, Step 4 is the most important step of the knowledgebase creation process, as this is where you provide the source of the content that is seeded in the knowledgebase.

Also, if you want to migrate an existing knowledgebase into a new knowledgebase service, this step needs to be blank. After the service is created, you can then import the knowledgebase content through the Settings section. I show you the flow in the coming chapters, when I deal with modifying the knowledgebase.

This source of the content can be as follows:

- **URL**—This URL should be a public URL with open access. Meaning that it should not require any authentication steps to access. The URL should have structured content, with a question and answer format. You can add multiple URLs, depending up the associated QnA Maker management tier you selected.

- **Document**—The document can be any file or product manual. This file should contain content as questions and answers. At the time of writing this chapter, .tsv, .pdf, .doc, .docx, and .xlsx are the supported file formats.

This URL or document content will be extracted by the service and will be added as questions and answers to the knowledgebase. This appears as a test index under the Azure search. You can also add question and answers manually. You can also export existing knowledgebases and import them to the newly created knowledgebase after creation. We will explore this flow in later parts of the book.

In this chapter, I use content from the Apress FAQ page. At the time of writing this chapter, the FAQ content from Apress was presented in a URL as `https://www.apress.com/in/services/faq`, as seen in Figure 3-5.

Figure 3-5. *The FAQ page added as the content source using an URL*

Step 4 presents with text to enter the URL and click the +Add URL link. Based on the pricing tier you selected, you can keep adding different URLs, by clicking the +Add URL link. In this chapter, I add only one URL, as mentioned.

Along with the URL, as a heads-up about using documents, I also created a sample document with four questions in a question and answer sequence. This can be seen in Figure 3-6.

Question and Answer Word document sample

What is this book all about?

This book is everything about QnA Maker service.

Who is the Author of this book?

Author for this book is Mr. Kasam Shaikh, Founder of Dear Azure, Leads az-INDIA community.

Does only Apress has published this book?

Yes

Do we have any other book with this topic in Market?

No, as of now we don't have any other book covering this amazing topic

Figure 3-6. *Sample document for adding a content source*

Files can be added by clicking the + Add file link presented in Step 4. Click the link and then browse the file from your system. This will add the file and list it in the Filename section from the web portal. Again, depending on your pricing tier, you can keep adding files with the supported format and structure.

You can also delete a file by clicking on the delete icon next to the file. Figure 3-7 shows the Apress FAQ URL being added, along with sample document.

STEP 4

Populate your KB.
Extract question-and-answer pairs from an online FAQ, product manuals, or other files. Supported formats are .tsv, .pdf, .doc, .docx, .xlsx, containing questions and answers in sequence. Learn more about knowledge base sources. Skip this step to add questions and answers manually after creation. The number of sources and file size you can add depends on the QnA service SKU you choose. Learn more about QnA Maker SKUs.

URL

https://www.apress.com/in/services/faq

http://

+ Add URL

File name

qnapress-doc.docx

+ Add file

Figure 3-7. *Step 4 of knowledgebase creation after adding the content source*

Step 5: Create Your Knowledgebase

The last step is to complete the feeding process and to proceed with knowledgebase creation. Click the Create Your KB button presented in Step 5, as shown in Figure 3-8.

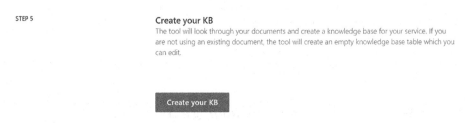

Figure 3-8. *Step 5 of knowledgebase creation*

Clicking on the Create Your KB button will go through all URLs and documents added in the previous steps and will create the knowledgebase. This can take a few minutes to complete, depending on your content. Figure 3-9 shows the wait message presented by the portal.

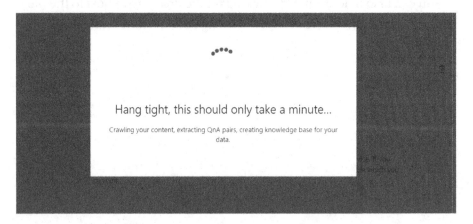

Figure 3-9. *Message shown upon clicking the Create Your KB button*

Once the content from all the sources is extracted, the portal navigates to the Knowledgebase Edit page. From this page, you can make further modifications to the knowledgebase.

As shown in Figure 3-10, the content is displayed in grid format with the column name as Question and Answer. The grid also specifies the original source of content. I had added one URL and one document. Question and Answer will be displayed in the same manner, with the source mentioned. The grid displays 10 rows per page and adds page numbers to the footer area. You can even collapse and expand rows grouped by each input source.

Figure 3-10. *Displaying extracted content from the input source after knowledgebase creation*

You can manually add multiple questions and answers using the same screen. If you look at Figure 3-10 again, you will notice a link called + Add QnA Pair in the top-right corner of the screen. Clicking this link will present you with an option to add pairs of questions and answers. In this chapter, I will add two random messages for my bot users. This manually added question set is grouped under the source name Editorial. Figure 3-11 shows the newly added greeting content in question and answer format.

- Question – "Hi" | Answer – "Welcome to Apress Bot!"

- Question – "I have a query" | Answer – "We are happy to help you with answering your queries."

Knowledge base

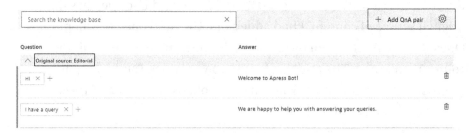

Figure 3-11. *Manually added question and answer set, grouped as Editorial*

I will explain how to update the knowledgebase in more detail in coming chapters. As of now, let's focus on creating a knowledgebase.

Save and Train

As mentioned earlier in this chapter about the lifecycle of a knowledgebase, the Save and Train action is the most important action you'll do. You use it to commit all additions, modifications, and deletions to your knowledgebase. No changes are reflected unless you click Save and Train. Refer to Figure 3-12.

Figure 3-12. *The link on the QnA Maker Web Portal to perform a Save and Train action*

In simple words, Save and Train saves the changes made to knowledgebase and trains the model to respond with the new changes.

As soon as you click the Save and Train button, in a few seconds, newly created content is saved to your knowledgebase. It is reflected within the Indexes section of the Azure search associated with your knowledgebase as `testkb`. Refer to Figure 3-13 to see the knowledgebase added to Azure search.

Figure 3-13. *The knowledgebase added to Azure search under Indexes in the Azure Portal*

In Figure 3-13, the Document Count is a total count of questions and answers extracted from a given document source and Storage Size is the size of the knowledgebase added.

Publishing the Knowledgebase

Publishing is the final step to make your knowledgebase live. Once it's published, the QnA content moves from the test index to the production index, in the associated Azure search service. It also enables RESTful endpoint to access the knowledgebase in the bot or application.

At the top menu bar, next to the Edit option, there is command for publishing a knowledgebase—it's aptly called Publish. Click on Publish to proceed. It will present you with the QnA service details and provide information about what you will achieve after publishing. Also, it presents you with information regarding your last publish effort. If it's the first time you have published a knowledgebase, it will display the message, "Your service has never been deployed". Refer to Figure 3-14.

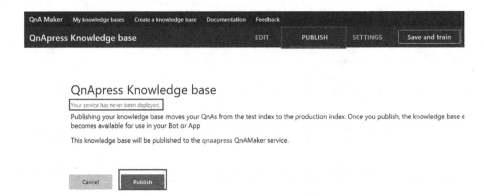

Figure 3-14. *The QnA Maker Portal screen after clicking Publish*

As you can see in Figure 3-15, clicking on Publish presents you with a RESTful knowledgebase endpoint. It also provides a sample HTTP request that needs to be triggered in order to get responses from the knowledgebase. We will explore this by integrating our QnA Maker knowledgebase service into the bot framework.

Success! Your service has been deployed. What's next?

You can always find the deployment details in your service's settings.

Use the below HTTP request to build your bot. Learn how.

Sample HTTP request	POST /knowledgebases/e38997d3-19ba-4ba6-b5ab-1e2bc0115285/generateAnswer Host: https://qnaapress.azurewebsites.net/qnamaker Authorization: EndpointKey 9a74dbb5-986e-418b-8817-04d41ffa31b6 Content-Type: application/json {"question":"<Your question>"}

Need to fine-tune and refine? Go back and keep editing your service.

Edit Service

Figure 3-15. *The knowledgebase endpoint details after publishing*

Let's look at that sample request carefully. It has three important parameters required for integrating the knowledgebase into any bot framework or for calling it from any application.

- **Knowledgbaseid**—GUID key referencing the knowledgebase.

- **Authorization key**—GUID authorization key for accessing the knowledgebase.

- **Host name**—App service URL, the runtime is being deployed.

Figure 3-16 shows QnA being moved to the production index from the test index at the associated Azure search. This movement confirms that our service is being published successfully.

Indexes

NAME	DOCUMENT COUNT	STORAGE SIZE
e38997d3-19ba-4ba6-b5ab-1e2bc0115285	24	26.2 KiB
testkb	24	23.48 KiB

Figure 3-16. *The Azure Portal displaying text index moved to production index for the associated Azure search*

Now you have two sets of knowledgebases. One is the testkb index and the other is the production index. So, when you want to make any additional changes to the knowledgebase and then Save and Train it, it will be added to the testkb index of the Azure search. And if you want to make the changes live for the outer world, you'll then have to publish them, as described here.

Summary

This is the end of the third chapter. This chapter described each step involved in creating a knowledgebase for your bot or application using the QnA Maker Web Portal. I also explained, with examples, how to use a document as the content source. You also saw how to add the content manually.

In the next chapter, I discuss the Azure Bot service and you learn how to integrate your knowledgebase into the Azure Bot service.

Happy Learning!

CHAPTER 4

Talk with Azure Bot Framework

In the last chapter, I talked about the bot backend, called the knowledgebase in the QnAMaker ecosystem. In that chapter, you created a knowledgebase from the Apress FAQ URL content source, which is a publicly available sample Word file with a few questions and answers. You also added a few questions and answers manually as a part of the Editorial section. And later, you learned how to make it public by publishing the knowledgebase and creating a RESTful endpoint to connect to it. In this chapter, you will see how to make the knowledgebase talk to the bot framework, which is the Azure Bot framework.

Recap: What Is a Bot?

A bot is an application or module that interacts with users in conversational ways or patterns. It could be an intelligent conversation, a trained pattern, or a request-response FAQ method. Bots include these phases:

- **Planning**—Planning revolves around why you need a bot. Consider the reason behind having your bot and the way your bot will behave with users when it's connected. In this chapter, we have the QnAMaker

© Kasam Shaikh 2019
K. Shaikh, *Developing Bots with QnA Maker Service*,
https://doi.org/10.1007/978-1-4842-4185-1_4

service extracting FAQs from the Apress public website. The bot will respond to the queries in a request-response fashion.

- **Building**—This includes the development environment, the technology stack, and the language used for bot development. They all play a vital role in making the bot function with ease. In this chapter, I will be using C# as the language and Visual Studio as the IDE.

- **Testing**—Like other complex applications, bots use many applications or modules working collectively and hence need a testing phase to ensure a bug-free experience.

- **Publishing**—The bot needs to be published to a local site or to a live environment by implementing continuous integration and deployment. I show discuss this implementation in a later chapter. In this chapter, you will learn how to publish the bot to the Azure Bot service.

- **Connecting**—Connecting the bot to social channels leads to increased interactions with the bot users and the target audience. In the coming chapters, I show you how to connect the bot with social channels like web channels, the Telegram app, etc.

- **Evaluating**—Data collected from the bot's interactions can help improve the performance and capabilities of the bot.

In order to transform our knowledgebase from backend data to the bot's brain, let's make it talk to the bot framework. In this chapter, you will explore the Azure Bot service in more detail.

The Azure Bot service provides an easy-to-follow tool that enables developers to pass their bots through all phases—build, test, publish, connect, and evaluate. It comes with predefined templates that are compatible with different programming languages. I explain this further later in this chapter, with details.

The Azure Web App Bot

To develop a bot, Microsoft Azure offers the Web App Bot service. It's a combination of web app and the initially offered bot service. It comes with an efficient Build Management section to work with. Let's start by creating the service and looking at it in detail.

Getting Started with Azure Web App Bot

I am using the Azure Bot service, and hence need an Azure subscription. I will be creating a Web App Bot service using the Microsoft Azure Portal.

1. Open the Azure Portal by visiting `http://www.portal.azure.com`.

2. Click on + New Resource and type **Web App Bot**. This will list the Web App Bot services categorized under "AI + Machine Learning," as shown in Figure 4-1.

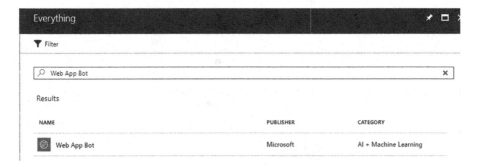

Figure 4-1. *Listing of the Web App Bot services on the Microsoft Azure Portal*

Once you select the service, it will present you with a
blade to provide a few details. Figure 4-2 presents the
blade with details.

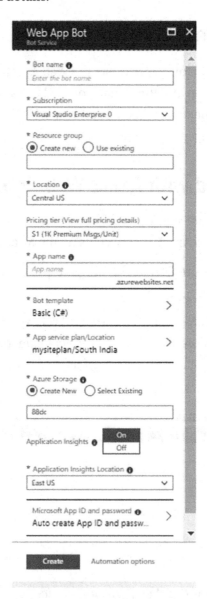

Figure 4-2. *This blade opens while creating the Azure Web App Bot*

Let's dive into the details:

- **Bot Name**—This will be your Web App Bot name. When you test the build, you'll build your knowledgebase with the Azure Bot service, this name will be used as a reference handle. It's mandatory to provide a name for your Web App Bot. You can also later change this name. In this chapter, I named it `qnapressbo`.

- **Subscription**—Web App Bot is the Azure resource, so you need an Azure subscription to access and leverage these features. You can use Azure Bot service with any available subscription, and even with a Azure free trial account. In this chapter, I use the Azure free trial subscription. This is to show that even using the free trial account, you can get your hands dirty working with the Azure Bot.

- **Resource Group**—As we are dealing with Azure resources, it's mandatory to connect to the logical grouping of resources, known as the resource group. You can create a new resource group or select from an existing on. In this chapter, I create a new resource group called `qnapressbot`.

- **Location**—You need to provide the location for the resource deployment once it's created. You can select from multiple available options. In this chapter, I use the one default selected, Central US.

- **Pricing Tier**—You need to go with any one tier from presented the pricing tiers. At the time of writing this book, Azure Bot service pricing tier offered two pricing tiers, as shown in Figure 4-3.

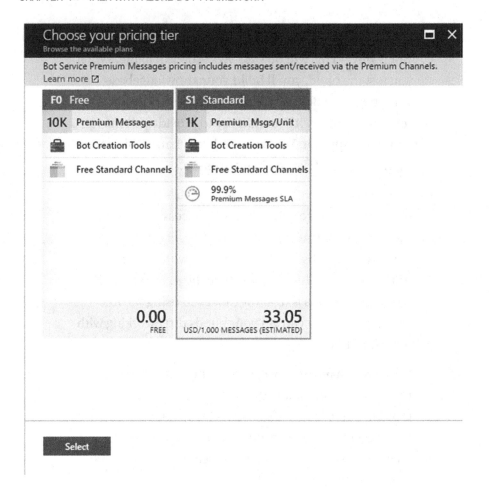

Figure 4-3. Pricing tiers presented for the Azure Web App Bot

a. Free – F0—This users to have 10K Premium messages, enabling the bot creation tools and allowing users to integrate with standard channels.

b. Standard – S1—Along with the free tier feature options, it also comes with two important advantages. First, it allows 1K premium messages per unit and provides 99.9% premium message SLA.

When I quote Bot service premium messages, it also includes messages sent/received via the premium channels involved. In this chapter, I select the Standard S1 as the pricing tier.

Select the tier you want and click the Select button.

- **App Name**—The App Service name will form your bot's endpoint URL, for example `<name-given>`. `azurewebsites.net`. As mentioned earlier in the chapter, this service is a combination of a web app and the bot. This name needs to be globally unique, as it forms a public URL. By default, it uses the bot name as the app name, if the site is available. You can change it, but not after you create the service.

  In this chapter, I keep this set to the same name as the bot, i.e., `qnapressbot`. So, my endpoint will be `qnapressbot.azurewebsite.com`.

- **Bot Template**—This is one of the most important options to set when creating your Azure Bot service. The bot template provides a simple starting point for your bot. See Figure 4-4.

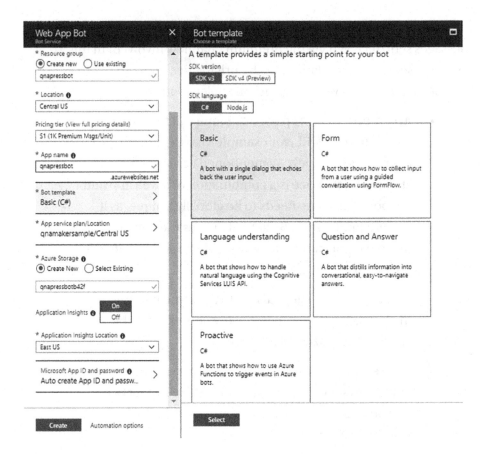

Figure 4-4. *The bot templates with available SDKs and supported languages*

At the time of this writing, it comes with two SDK templates:

a. **SDK v3 Version 3**—Comes with five supportive templates, for both the C# and Node.js programming languages.

b. **SDK v4 (Preview)**—At the time of this writing, version 4 is in preview and supports only one template for both supportive languages, as shown in Figure 4-5.

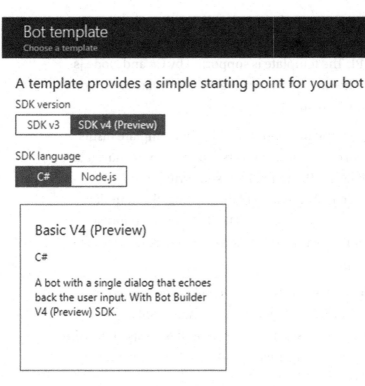

Figure 4-5. *Languages and templates supported by SDK v4 (preview)*

At the time of this writing, there are five templates presented for use with the Azure Bot service:

a. **Basic**—This bot template comes with a single dialog that echoes back the user input. The Template is supported by C# and Node.js. This is the only template supported by SDK v4 and SDK v3.

b. **Form**—This bot template collects input from the users using a guided conversation. It uses FormFlow to manage forms when used with C# and uses waterfalls when used with Node.js. This template is supported by C# and Node.js. At the time of this writing, this template is supported only by SDK v3.

c. **Language Understanding**—This template handles natural languages using the Cognitive Services LUIS API. The template is supported by C# and Node.js. At the time of this writing, this template is supported only by SDK v3.

d. **Question and Answer**—This bot template distils information into conversational, easy-to-navigate answers. The template is supported by C# and Node.js. At the time of this writing, this template is supported only by SDK v3. I use this template to connect with the QnAMaker service later in this chapter.

e. **Proactive**—This template helps you use Azure functions to trigger events in Azure bots. The template is supported by C# and Node.js. At the time of this writing, this template is supported only by SDK v3.

- **App Service Plan/Location**—This plan is associated with the web app being created with the service. The pricing tier currently defaults to the standard S1 tier. You can change the plan after the resource is created. You can also select from existing app service plans associated with your Azure subscription. The same goes for the resource location. In this chapter, I create a new app service plan name called QnApress and select the location as East US. The App Service Creation blade is shown in Figure 4-6.

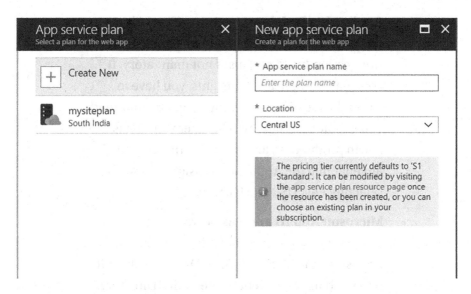

Figure 4-6. *The option to select from an existing app service plan or to create a new plan*

- **Azure Storage**—While creating an Azure Bot service, it's mandatory to create a storage account supporting blobs, queues, and table storage. This can be used to store the bot state. The Azure Bot framework enables you to store state data associated with users during conversion. This state could be anything, such as a context during a conversation or the user preferences. This data could be stored in table storage, SQL, or CosmosDB. You can create a new storage account or select from an existing one from your subscription. In this chapter, I am creating a new storage account called `strqnapressbot`.

- **Application Insights/Location**—This helps
  you enable analytics for your bot via the Azure
  Application Insights. This is not man atory. If
  you enable Application Insights, you have to
  select the location for deploying it. I recommend
  you enable it, as it helps a lot after your bot is
  live in production, and hence, in this chapter, I
  am enabling the Application Insights option and
  selecting East US as its location.

- **Microsoft App ID and Password**—This option
  is not mandatory, as by default it automatically
  provisions the Microsoft App ID and the default
  password in the current Azure Active Directory. You
  can also manually create one at the Microsoft App
  Registration Portal, as seen in Figure 4-7. In this
  chapter, I go with the default auto-creation option.

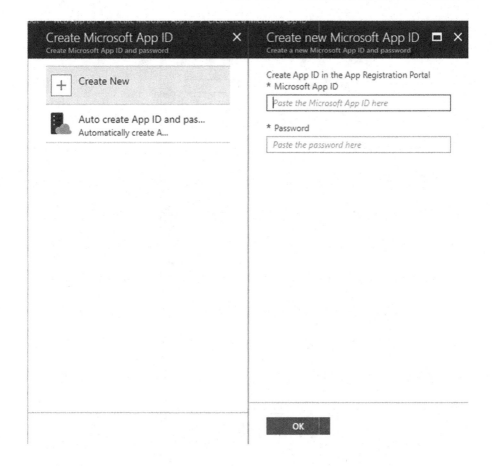

Figure 4-7. *Manually creating an ID/password using the Microsoft App Registration Portal*

Figure 4-8 shows the Azure Web App Bot registration blade after providing all details explained in this section. Click Create to initiate service deployment.

Figure 4-8. *The Azure Web App Bot registration blade with details*

The process will take a few minutes to create and deploy all required resources. You will be notified by the Azure Portal once the deployment process is complete.

You can navigate to the newly created service using the resource option on the left side of the navigation panel over the screen or using the button that appears with notification.

Click on the Resource group called qnapressbot. You can see all the new resources listed, as shown in Figure 4-9. Along with the Web App Bot App service, the Application Insights and storage account are created.

NAME	TYPE	LOCATION	
qnapressbot	Web App Bot	global	...
qnapressbot	App Service	East US	...
qnapressbota5ipeb	Application Insights	East US	...
strqnapressbot	Storage account	Central US	...

Figure 4-9. *The Azure resources created along with the Azure Web App Bot*

Let's choose the Web App Bot resource, qnapressbot.

Here you can see well define sections for managing bot phases, as mentioned earlier in this chapter. In Figure 4-10 you can observe the sections related to the Web App Bot Azure service.

It comes with the following sections:

- **General Section**—This section helps to explore overview details of the service, such as its name, subscription, etc. Access control and service activity logs with tags are presented in this section as well.

- **Bot Management** —All phases under bot development are part of this section. You can build the bot, test it with a live backend, connect it to social channels, monitor the analytics, and even change the bot pricing tier from this section. We utilize this section in a later part of this chapter, in order to integrate it with the QnAMaker knowledgebase. I also explain how to connect the bot to other social channels using the Bot Management section.

- **App Service Settings**—This section mainly deals with configuring keys and other application-related settings.

- **Support**—All new support requests pertaining to service are managed under this section.

Figure 4-10. *Web App Bot service blade*

Integrating with the QnAMaker Knowledgebase

In the last chapter, we created a QnAMaker knowledgebase, the backend or brain of our bot. Now we created the Azure Bot service to bring our bot into action.

First, we need to make our Azure Bot talk to the QnAMaker knowledgebase. Here we need to provide three important parameters from the QnAMaker knowledgebase to the Azure Bot service.

Navigate to the Application Settings under the App Service Settings section of the Web App Bot service blade. You'll see list of app settings listed in tabular format.

All the configuration settings parameters for Azure storage, Application Insights, bot IDs, and bot environments are listed in the application setting as the app setting name and value. You can use this information to implement the same in your application. Even the Microsoft App ID and Microsoft App password that I use for auto-creation is shown in this section.

If you remember that I selected bot template as question and answer, an additional three app setting names are presented:

- QnAAuthKey

- QnAEndpointHostName

- QnAKnowledgebaseId

With the corresponding value set to blank. You need to provide these parameters in order to integrate the QnAMaker knowledgebase with the Azure Bot service. You have these three values in the QnAMaker Portal.

Reading QnAMaker Parameters

Open the QnAMaker Web Portal from http://qnamaker.ai/ and click the My Knowledge Base section on the top menu bar.

You will be presented with all the knowledgebase service you created. In last chapter, I created a QnAMaker knowledgebase service called QnApress Knowledge Base. You can see it listed here.

Click on the View Code link presented with the knowledgebase, highlighted in Figure 4-11.

Figure 4-11. *Viewing the code from the QnAMaker Portal*

This will open a popup screen presenting a Sample HTTP Request that will allow you to talk to the QnAMaker knowledgebase. Check the request carefully, as it presents you with all three required parameters of the Azure Bot service app settings. The parameters are shown in Figure 4-12.

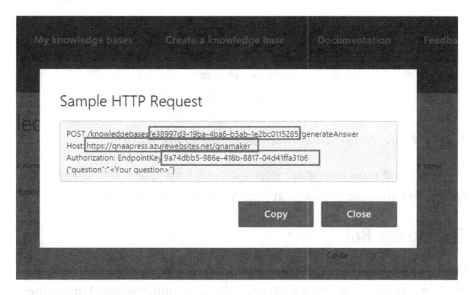

Figure 4-12. *Sample HTTP request with the required values highlighted*

Copy these values and paste them into the respective boxes under the Value column in the App Settings section in the Azure Portal, as shown in Figure 4-13.

Figure 4-13. *Key parameters added in the app service settings*

I recommend you check Figures 4-12 and 4-13 so you're crystal clear in understanding the HTTP request and its associated values.

Once you've added the values, click on Save. It will take a few seconds to apply the given app settings. You'll be notified in the Notifications window in the Azure Portal, as shown in Figure 4-14.

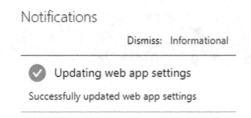

Figure 4-14. *Notification message on applying settings*

This is the most important step to connect, associate, and integrate the QnAMaker knowledgebase with your Azure Web App Bot service.

Testing the Bot

Once you're done with the integration process, it's time to test the bot. To do so, Azure Web App Bot services has the provision presented under the Bot Management section.

Navigate to the Test in Web Chat section under Bot Management. Here you will be presented with a chat window echoing the Real Chat interface. I entered a few questions from the knowledgebase to test the response.

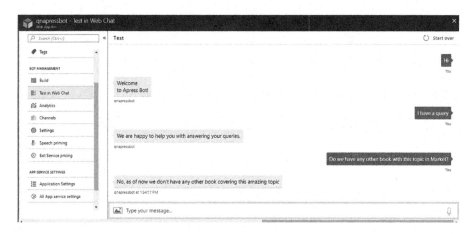

Figure 4-15. *Chat in the Test window in the Azure Portal*

This test resulted in 100% successful responses, as shown in Figure 4-15.

Summary

The chapter explained the Microsoft Azure offering for your bot service. You learned about the creation process and other Azure resources associated with it. I further explained the bot templates that you should choose when developing the QnAMaker Bot.

In next the chapter, I show you how to connect the bot to live social channels. I also implement continuous integration and continuous deployment to publish the bot live to a public URL.

I recommend that you dive in with this implementation and be ready to take the bot live to the outer world.

Until then, Happy Learning!

CHAPTER 5

Connecting FAQ Bot to Social Channels

In the last chapter, I explained the Azure Bot framework offering, called the Web App Bot service. We created and integrated QnA Maker knowledgebase into the Azure Bot service. In this chapter, I explain how to connect the bot to social channels.

Available Social Channels

You must be aware of the power of social channels. You can double your audience reach with the help of social channels. They help you get easily connected to your target audience, more easily meeting your business requirements for bot development.

Consider you own Facebook page for selling an online product. You developed a product FAQ bot and integrated it with your Facebook messenger. Imagine the ease of response and the wider customer reach you may receive by implementing this.

Similarly, say you are running a campaign via an SMS medium. You want your incoming SMS to respond to the user or participant with a required answer. Here, you develop a bot, and your bot is handling the said flow. Your campaign will be boosted to the next level!

© Kasam Shaikh 2019
K. Shaikh, *Developing Bots with QnA Maker Service*,
https://doi.org/10.1007/978-1-4842-4185-1_5

Interesting! There are many such use cases, wherein you or your organization would benefit from having connected to social channels.

The Azure Bot Service presents you with an easy interface in the Azure portal to get your bot connected to social channels. In the Service blade, under Bot Management, there is a section named Channels. Navigate to this section under Bot Management to find all the available social channels.

At the time of writing this chapter, there are 12 social channels supported to get connected via the Azure Bot Service, four of which are listed as Featured channels. They are:

- Cortana

- Direct Line

- Microsoft Teams

- Skype

Other channels available include these:

- Facebook Messenger

- GroupMe

- Kik

- Skype for Business

- Slack

- Telegram

- Twilio (SMS)

- Web Chat

By default, Azure Bot is already connected to the Web Chat channel. Let's connect our bot to one of the available channels.

Connecting the Bot to Telegram

Every channel has its own way to talk with Azure Bot. The authentication and authorization processes differ from channel to channel. In this chapter, I show you the process of connecting Azure Bot to Telegram, a cloud-based instant messaging service used globally.

To connect the channel, you have to open the Microsoft Azure Portal in any browser.

1. Open the Web App Bot resource we created in the last chapter.

2. On the Service blade, under Bot Management, click the Channel section. Here you will be presented with the available social channels. Click on the channel icon you want your bot to connect to. In my case, it's Telegram.

3. This will present you with an interface to provide an access token. This token comes with the bot you create in the Telegram app. You need to create a bot in Telegram and provide the account access token on the Azure Bot Service blade. This will enable the Azure Bot Service to talk to the Telegram app.

4. Now generate the access token and install Telegram in your mobile. Once it's installed, search for BotFather. This bot will help you create and mange your own bot in Telegram. See Figure 5-1.

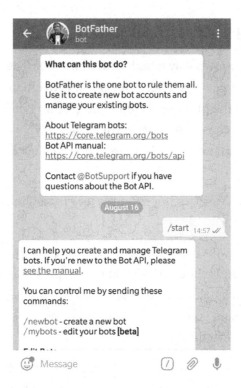

Figure 5-1. *The BotFather bot mobile interface in the Telegram app*

5. It presents you with command instructions to create
    and manage your bot in Telegram. To start with,
    follow these steps:

    - Write /newbot and press Enter. It will ask you to
      provide a name for your bot. Provide the bot name
      as per your requirements. In this chapter, I used the
      name Apress.

    - Once you provide the name, it will ask you to enter
      a username for your bot. This should be globally
      unique and must end with bot. In this chapter,
      I provided the username qnamakerbykasambot.

6. Once you're done with the previous step, BotFather
    presents a greeting message and provides the following:

    •   An URL to open the newly created bot

    •   An access token, which is a combination of a
        numeric value, a colon, and a GUID

Figure 5-2 shows the step-by-step instructions.

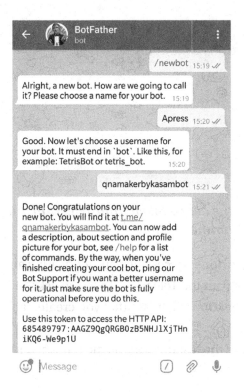

Figure 5-2. *Steps followed to generate the access token*

7. Once the token is generated, copy the token
    carefully and paste it in the required text box on the
    Azure Portal screen, as shown in Figure 5-3.

8. Click on Save.

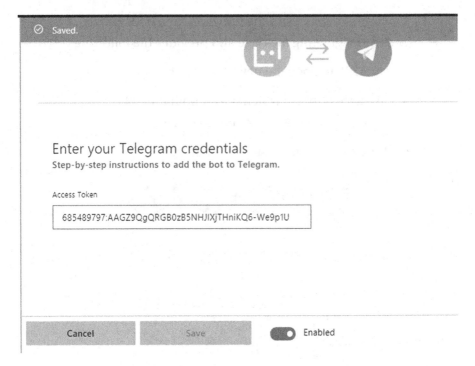

Figure 5-3. *Copy the access token from Telegram and paste it here, in the Azure Portal Channel section*

That's it! You are done successfully authenticating and authorizing Azure Web App Bot with the Telegram. To test it, ask the same questions from the QnA Maker knowledgebase that you created and verify the response.

Figure 5-4 shows the test message as the request and response is being received.

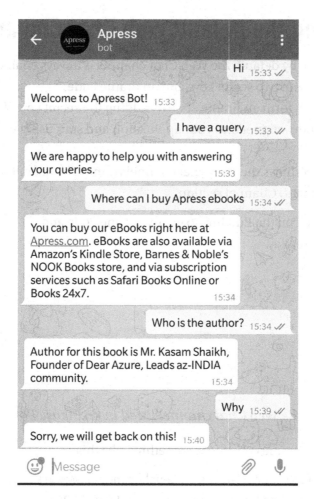

Figure 5-4. *Request and response via the Telegram app*

Note   The bot profile picture seen in Figure 5-4 is being added through the command instructions in the Telegram app.

So, here you successfully connected the FAQ Bot Azure Bot Service with the social channel, Telegram. Simple, isn't it? It's smart to try these steps to connect your own bot with Telegram. Not only Telegram, but try it with other channels as well.

Exploring the Default Web Chat Channel

As mentioned, by default, the Web Chat channel is always enabled. It presents you with two secret keys and an iframe code.

You have to form an Iframe code by adding the secret key. Now, place this iframe code snippet into your application and start using your FAQ bot!

Figure 5-5 shows the Web Chat channel running by default under the Bot Management, Channel section.

1. Click on the Edit link to get the iframe code and secret key.

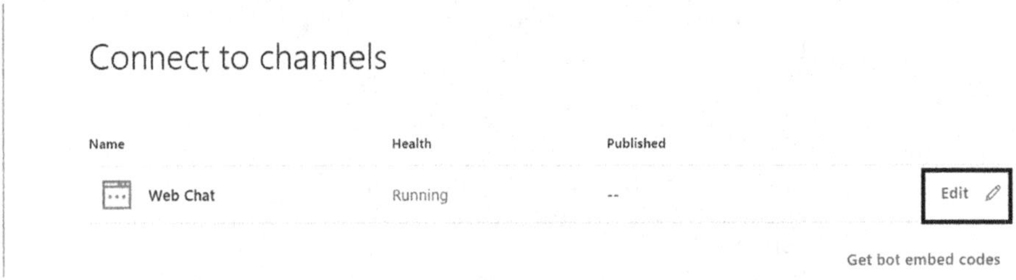

Figure 5-5. *The Web Chat channel listed in the Azure Portal*

The iframe code looks something like this:

```
<iframe src='https://webchat.botframework.
com/embed/qnapressbot?s=YOURSECRETHERE'>
</iframe>
```

2. You need to add the secret key to the iframe code.

3. Secret keys will be presented once you click on the Edit link. Figure 5-6 depicts the secret key presented by the Web Chat channel. You can regenerate this key, in case your key gets compromised. Just click on the Regenerate link.

4. These keys come with a mask over them. You need to click on the Show link to display the actual key.

Configure Web Chat

+ Add new site	Default Site ✎		☐ Disable	🗑
Default Site	**Secret keys**		
	XXXXXXXXXXXXXXXXXXXXXXXXXXXXXXXX	Show	Regenerate
	XXXXXXXXXXXXXXXXXXXXXXXXXXXXXXXX	Show	Regenerate
	Embed code		
	<iframe		
Done			

Figure 5-6. *Secret keys presented by the Web Chat channel*

5. Now, add this iframe code in plain HTML, as shown in Figure 5-7. This iframe code is generic, with changes in the query string parameters, depending upon the bot name and subscription key.

```
index.html  ⊕ ✕
 1    <html>
 2    <head>
 3        <meta charset="utf-8" />
 4        <title> Apress Bot - By Kasam Shaikh</title>
 5    </head>
 6    <body>
 7        <h1>Apress FAQ Bot</h1>
 8        <br />
 9
10    <iframe height="600" width="500"
11            src='https://webchat.botframework.com/embed/qnapressbot?s=5UgabK3G1EH.cwA.Kwc.1uXHeq3-8U8pJTAGSO9ee1tBMUgmLZwZYiMJI-S8ASg'>
12    </iframe>
13        <br />
14        <br />
15        <h5>Note: This Bot is for demo purpose only - Kasam Shaikh ( @KasamShaikh | @dearazure_net )</h5>
16    </body>
17    </html>
18
19
```

Figure 5-7. *Simple HTML code adding the Web Chat iframe code*

6.   Open the HTML in a browser. Make sure you are
     connected to the Internet. You will notice a Web
     Chat window.

7.   Now try a few questions from the QnA Maker
     knowledgebase to verify a successful connection.

Observe Figure 5-8 carefully. The request and response coming into
Web Chat is exactly the same as the way it responded in the Telegram app.

Apress FAQ Bot

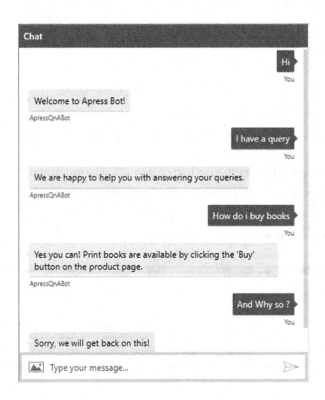

Figure 5-8. *Web Chat in HTML form with a request-response
message from QnA Maker*

Deleting a Connected Channel

The Azure Bot Service, Bot Management Channel section allows you to delete connected channels with ease. It displays a button called Delete Channel for all connected channels except for the Web Chat channel.

1. Click the Delete Channel button. It prompts you with a confirmation message.

2. Confirm your action and you are done!

As I connected my bot to the Telegram app, I will delete the same. All I need to do is click on the Delete Channel button and confirm my action. See Figure 5-9.

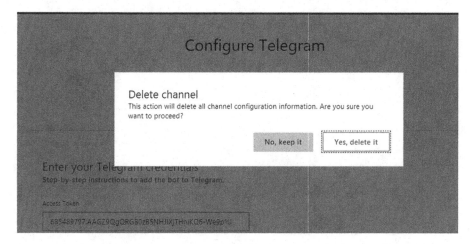

Figure 5-9. *Confirmation message received upon clicking Delete Channel*

Summary

In this chapter, I explained the steps to connect to the default Web Chat channel and Telegram app from among the available social channels. I verified the successful connection with the same sets of questions asked of the QnA Maker knowledgebase, both with the Web Chat channel and the

Telegram app. Also, I explained how to delete these connected channels, all using the Azure Portal.

In the coming chapter, we will explore the Build section under Bot Management. Will use the Web Chat channel HTML code to implement Continuous Integration and Continuous Deployment, which will demo the ease of bot development.

I recommend that you follow the chapter with connecting your bot with different social channels.

Happy Learning!

CHAPTER 6

Bot Build Management

Hello reader, I hope you have connected your bot to any of available social channels using QnA Maker and the Azure Web App Bot service, as I explained in the last chapter. If you have, congratulations, as your bot is a hero in the outer world and you are now a bot expert! If you have not done this yet, then never mind, just start using QnA Maker and the Azure Web App Bot to create your own FAQ Bot. You can get connected to the wider audience through social channels later.

This chapter explains all about bot build management. I shows you how to build an online bot using the Online Code Editor and do it offline using an IDE. In my case, it's Visual Studio 2017 v15.3. Also, I show you how to implement continuous deployment for your FAQ Bot.

Building a Bot Online

Figure 6-1 presents the way to work with bot development code. Using these ways, you can make the bot development process easy. You can go with any of the options presented here and keep upgrading your bot with the latest updates.

This section falls under Bot Management in the Azure Web App Bot.

© Kasam Shaikh 2019
K. Shaikh, *Developing Bots with QnA Maker Service*,
https://doi.org/10.1007/978-1-4842-4185-1_6

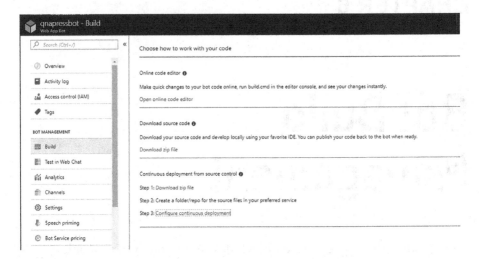

Figure 6-1. *Ways to work with bot code in the Azure Portal*

Using the Online Code Editor

Using this option, you can make quick changes to your bot code online. Yes, you can make changes to bot code online! You can also build your bot code online, which will reflect changes instantly, all by using the Online Code Editor presented by the Azure Web App Bot, from the Build section under Bot Management.

In this chapter, I show you how to make changes to your bot code and then build the code online. In Chapter 3, I mentioned the default response message sent by QnA Maker. If the requested query or input doesn't match the knowledgebase content, the default response message is "No good match in FAQ," as shown in Figure 6-2. Now this seems to be a very generic and dull message that's not too helpful either.

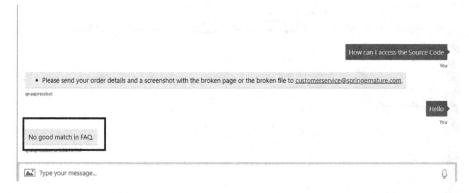

Figure 6-2. *The default response message by QnA Maker in the Test Chat window in the Azure Portal*

You can customize this message as needed, so that it suits your bot's purpose. I will show you how to change this default message. For this customization, you have to make a few changes to the bot code. I will make these changes to the bot code using the Online Code Editor.

Changing the Bot Code Online

Open the Web App Bot Service blade and click on the Build section under Bot Management. There, you will be presented with ways of working with your bot code options, as detailed at the beginning of this chapter. Select the Online Code Editor option. Refer to Figure 6-1 for better navigation.

This will open a new tab or window, presenting you with the following options, shown in Figure 6-3.

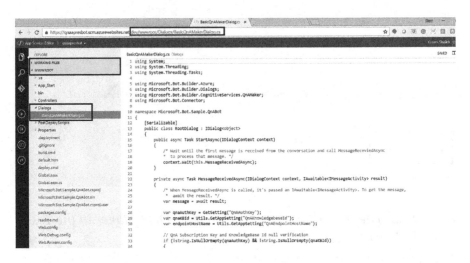

Figure 6-3. *The Online Code Editor*

The Code Editor uses the same authorization as your Azure Portal. If you notice the URL carefully, it has opened your App service URL and added scm. This opens the wwwroot folders with all the bot application files. You can go ahead and open any files presented there and make changes as required. The Code Editor comes with an Auto Saved implementation, which means as you make changes to the code, they are automatically saved.

To change the default response message, we need to make changes to the BasicQnAMakerDialog.cs file. This file can be viewed from the wwwroot/Dialogs/ directory. You can view the exact location of file highlighted in Figure 6-3.

Once you locate the file, head to its constructor method.

Here is the code snippet for the QnAMaker service, constructor method:

```
[Serializable]
public class BasicQnAMakerDialog : QnAMakerDialog
    {
```

```
public BasicQnAMakerDialog() : base(new
QnAMakerService(new QnAMakerAttribute(RootDialog.
GetSetting("QnAAuthKey"), Utils.GetAppSetting("QnAKnowl
edgebaseId"), "No good match in FAQ.", 0.5, 1, Utils.Ge
tAppSetting("QnAEndpointHostName")))))
{ }
}
```

Read this code snippet carefully. I have highlighted the default text being passed in the constructor method (remember that it's "No good match in FAQ."). You can also observe the three parameters— QnAKnowledgebaseId, QnAAuthKey, and QnAEndpointHostName—that we provided to the Azure Web App Bot under the application settings, which are being read here in this method.

Change the highlighted text to the message you want QnA Maker to display. Let's make the message, "Will get back to you, from the Online Editor".

```
,
[Serializable]
public class BasicQnAMakerDialog : QnAMakerDialog
    {
        public BasicQnAMakerDialog() : base(new
        QnAMakerService(new QnAMakerAttribute(RootDialog.
        GetSetting("QnAAuthKey"), Utils.GetAppSetting("QnAKnow
        ledgebaseId"), "Will get back to you, from the Online
        Editor.", 0.5, 1, Utils.GetAppSetting("QnAEndpointHostN
        ame")))))
        { }
}
```

Once you're done making code changes, as mentioned earlier, you don't have to do anything extra, as the changes are automatically saved.

Spinning Up the Bot Code

Now we are done making the required changes to the bot code online. But it doesn't end here. To reflect the changes you made, you need to spin up the bot code. In other words, we need to build the bot code. This is the same as when you make changes to your application code—you build the code to push it to further environments. Here, it's not as easy as clicking Start Build in your IDE. However, comparatively, it is much easier than building code with your bot code online.

It takes one click and one command to build your bot code online. You use the same page seen in Figure 6-3.

On the left side of the navigation pane, you find a rectangular icon listed in the second-to-last position from the bottom. If you mouse-over the icon, you will see the Open Console message. Click on the icon to open the Console window on the Online Editor.

Alternatively, you can open the console by pressing Ctrl+Shift+C from the keyboard.

Now in the Console window, enter this command:

```
build.cmd
```

This command will build your code and, in a few seconds, it will present you with message saying that the build was successful.

Figure 6-4 shows the icon, the Console window, and the `build` command highlighted.

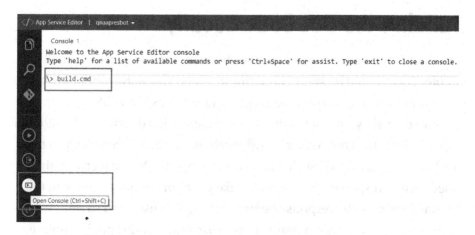

Figure 6-4. *Presenting the console icon, the shortcut keys, and the build command*

Once the success message is flashed on the screen, it's done!

Verify your change by navigating to the Test window under Bot Management. Input any random message to check the default response. Refer to Figure 6-5 for the request-response message.

Figure 6-5. *Changes verified in the Test window in the Azure Portal*

It's simple and interesting to work with your bot code online using the Online Code Editor presented by the Azure Web App Bot service. You can very well use this method to make instant changes with instant and productive results.

Building the Bot Code Locally

The changes you need to make to your bot code won't always be small and simple. There could be some scenarios in which you want your bot to talk with other third-party components or other services like LUIS.

Say you want your bot to talk to your database if it doesn't find a suitable response from the QnA Maker knowledgebase. In such a scenario, you need to add the code part to first check the response from QnA Maker, and then based on that response, you want to make your bot communicate with the database, validate the response before pushing it to user, and so on.

In such cases, it's not possible to perform entire code changes online. Here the best and recommended approach is to make code changes and the build locally.

The Azure Web App Bot => Bot Management => Build section presents you with options to download the source code locally. You can download the code, open it with your favorite IDE, build it locally, and then publish it back to the cloud, where the changes will be reflected to the outer world.

We will not make significant changes to the bot code, but will consider the same use case that we used previously—changing the default message. But this time we'll do it locally.

Navigate to the Build section and click on the second presented option, Download Zip File. It will take a few seconds to zip your bot files and folders. Once it's done, the portal will present you with a Download Zip File button. See Figure 6-6.

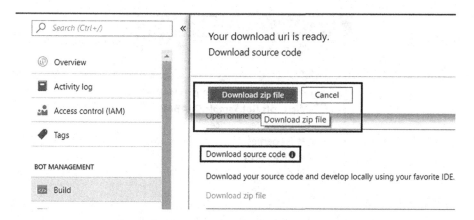

Figure 6-6. *Portal presenting the download link for the bot application's code*

Click on the link to download the folder. It's downloaded as a ZIP file, so you need to extract it first and then open it with your favorite IDE for .NET.

Note   We selected the template with the C# language, hence, .NET IDE is supported.

In this chapter, I will be using Visual Studio 2017 Community Edition as my IDE to open the bot application that we downloaded from the Azure Portal.

This will open the application files, with the same structure used in the Online Editor, under the wwwroot folder.

Open the same page—BasicQnAMakerDialog.cs under the Dialogs folder. Then, move to the constructor method code. Refer to Figures 6-7 and 6-8 to see how this is done.

Figure 6-7. *Bot application project files in Visual Studio 2017*

```
// Dialog for QnAMaker GA service
[Serializable]
public class BasicQnAMakerDialog : QnAMakerDialog
{
    // Go to https://qnamaker.ai and feed data, train & publish your QnA Knowledgebase.
    // Parameters to QnAMakerService are:
    // Required: qnaAuthKey, knowledgebaseId, endpointHostName
    // Optional: defaultMessage, scoreThreshold[Range 0.0 - 1.0]
    public BasicQnAMakerDialog() : base(new QnAMakerService(new QnAMakerAttribute(RootDialog.GetSetting("QnAAuthKey"),
        Utils.GetAppSetting("QnAKnowledgebaseId"), "Will get back to you, from Online Editor", 0.5, 1, Utils.GetAppSetting("QnAEndpointH
    { }
}
}
```

Figure 6-8. *Code block opened locally*

Note   You may notice in the commented section in Figure 6-8 that the code is called the QnA Maker GA service. GA stands for Generally Available. QnA Maker was announced as GA in May 2018. There are two code blocks, one for preview and one for GA. The preview part will be deprecated as of November 2018, and hence it's not mentioned explicitly.

Now make some changes to the default message here, so as to push and test it live, after deployment.

Let's make the new message "Will get back to you, from local!". Once you're done with the code changes, it's time to build and publish the code.

Build your code the way you do using your IDE. I built my code using the build command in Visual Studio 2017, and it was built successfully.

To publish the code, right-click on Project in the Solution Explorer and choose Publish, as shown in Figure 6-9.

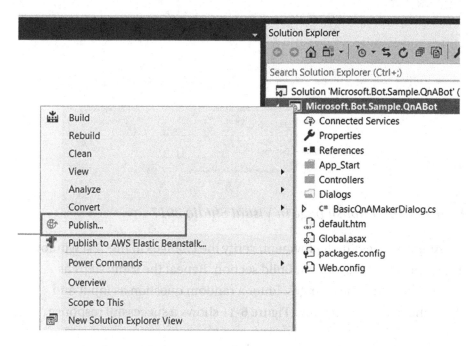

Figure 6-9. *The Publish to Web App option in Solution Explorer, Visual Studio 2017*

As shown in Figure 6-10, this will present you with a Publish page in Visual Studio 2017, with the web app details it was downloaded from. Choose Publish to deploy the code to Azure. Follow the instructions that appear during the deployment process. I will not discuss the steps to deploy files to Azure using Visual Studio 2017, as it's not in the scope of the book to do so. You can refer to the documentation provided by Microsoft Visual Studio, which details the steps, at `https://docs.microsoft.com/en-us/visualstudio/deployment/tutorial-import-publish-settings-azure?view=vs-2017`.

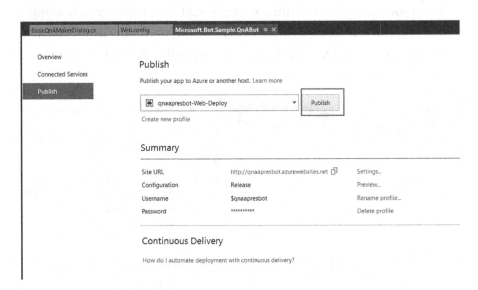

Figure 6-10. *Publish page in Visual Studio 2017*

After a successful deployment, verify the changes in the Test window under the Bot Management, Build section. Repeat the same steps as previous to verify the changes. Enter a random question as input and check the response message. Figure 6-11 shows a successful response.

Figure 6-11. *Changes verified in the Test window in the Azure Portal*

Figure 6-11 confirms that our code was successfully changed locally, built locally, and published back to the bot, ready to use live!

Continuous Deployment

Another important way to work with bot code presented by the Azure Bot service is by implementing continuous deployment from the source control. It comes with three easy steps:

1. Download the ZIP file. Here I will be using a plain HTML file with embedded Web Chat iframe code.

2. Create a folder/repo for the source files in your preferred service. Here, I will create repo in my GitHub account.

3. Configure continuous deployment.

In an earlier chapter, while connecting our FAQ Bot to a web chat, I used a simple HTML file to add the web chat iframe code. I will use the same HTML file and add it to my GitHub account. In this chapter, I created a repository named ApressBot in my GitHub account and added the HTML file into the repo, as seen in Figure 6-12.

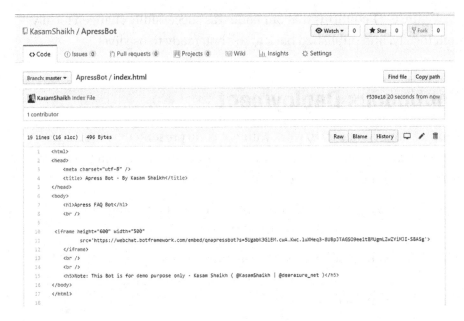

Figure 6-12. *GitHub repository with an index file added*

Now, going back to the Azure Portal, open the Web App Bot Service blade => Bot Management => Build section. Here the third option presented is of implementing continuous deployment. Skip Step 1, as we are using our own file. Click the link shown in Step 3.

Link will present you with a blade in the Azure Portal with deployment option details. If you are doing this for the first time, it displays a message saying "No deployments found". It also presents an option to configure the Deployment option. Refer to Figure 6-13.

Figure 6-13. *Deployments Option blade in the Azure Portal*

You can choose from the available source control options with Azure. At the time of writing this book, the source repositories options that were available are shown in **Figure 6-14.**

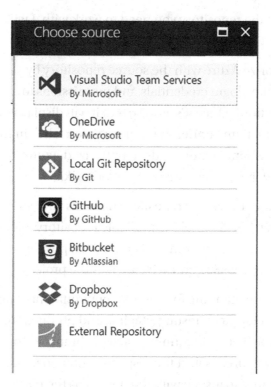

Figure 6-14. *Source Control options available in Azure for configuring continuous deployment*

In this chapter, as mentioned earlier, I will be using GitHub as the source.

You need to authorize your account with the source you are going to use. You need to authorize the talk between Azure and your source repository. Configure your source with the following steps:

1. Select the repository you need to work with. I will select GitHub from the list.

2. Authorize Azure with the source repository by providing login credentials and permissions to a few actions. Once it's authorized, it will display your account name under the Authorization label, in the Deployment Option blade. I authorized Azure with my GitHub account named KasamShaikh.

3. You have to select a repository name as your source project. It will list all the available repository folders from your source control. I created a repository called ApressBot and selected it as the project.

4. If you are planning for different environments, such as development, testing, staging, and production, and you want environment-specific branches to be configured, select the respective branch name. You can also just go with the default as the master branch, which is what I do here.

5. We don't configure the Performance Test option in this example.

6. Once you're done with all the steps, click OK.

The configurations you just went through are all reflected in Figure 6-15.

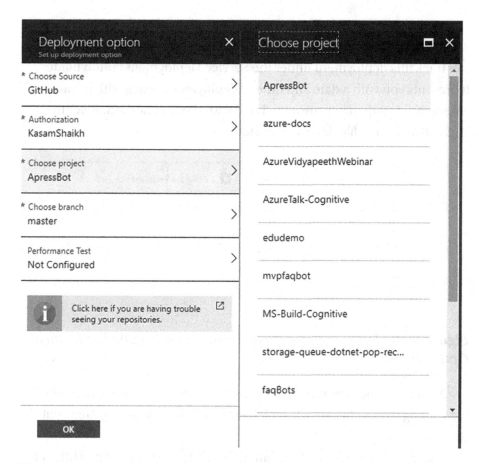

Figure 6-15. *Deployment options configuration steps in the Azure Portal*

As soon as you click OK, Azure will fetch all the files from the configured repository and deploy them to the associated web app. You can track this deployment under the Service Deployment option blade. It presents you with a date and time of deployment, along with file and comments details, if any are associated with the file check-in. Refer to Figure 6-16 for my file deployment status.

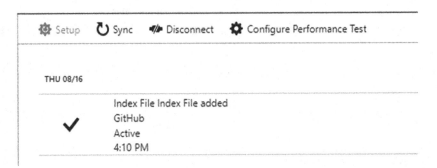

Figure 6-16. *Deployment status presented in the Azure Deployment Option blade*

Notice the Index as the filename and the time set as the deployment date, along with a checkmark, which indicates that the deployment status was successful.

You can also verify the deployment by navigating to the App URL in a browser. Navigate to https://qnapressbot.azurewebsites.in/index. html. Refer to Figure 6-17.

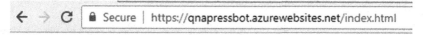

Apress FAQ Bot

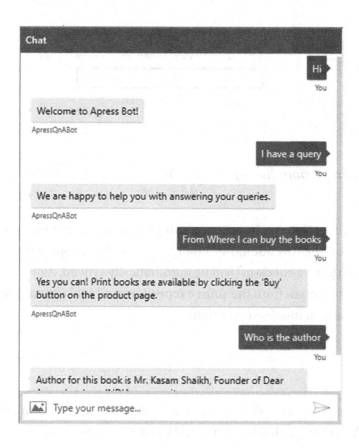

Note: This Bot is for demo purpose only - Kasam Shaikh (@KasamShaikh | @dearazure_net)

Figure 6-17. *An HTML page live on a public web app URL with the Web Chat and Apress FAQ Bot*

Also, once the deployment option is configured, it can be seen, as shown in Figure 6-18. The configured source control details are presented in the Build section.

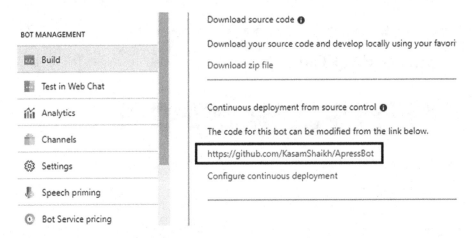

Figure 6-18. *This section displays the configured source control details*

This also confirms that you have successfully implemented continuous deployment to your bot. Any additional changes you make to your code (as long as you perform a check-in) will be automatically synced. Azure will sync the latest changes from the source repository and make them live instantly without any manual intervention.

Summary

In this chapter, I explained the development activities you can perform on your bot code. You learned that you can build the bot code both online and offline. For quick and minor changes, it's best to work and build online. And with development activities involving wider scope changes, it's best to perform the task locally and then push it to the bot in a few clicks. Also, I discussed implementing continuous deployment to republish the code to Azure whenever you make a code change to your source control service. In the next chapter, you will work more with the QnA Maker knowledgebase. You will explore its edit settings and testing capabilities.

Happy Learning!

CHAPTER 7

Things You Must Know About the QnAMaker Knowledgebase

As we are going to explore the QnAMaker service, which is part of Azure Cognitive services, it's good to build context around the Azure cognitive services first. By this time, you should have your very own FAQ Bot developed using the Cognitive QnAMaker service, with a QnAMaker knowledgebase connected to different social channels. If not, I recommend that you have one. This chapter explains how to deal with the QnAMaker knowledgebase post-production deployment of your bot. In the last chapter, I presented the build management activities associated with your bot application code, both online and offline, but for a smart and efficient bot, we need the knowledgebase to be up to date.

You must work by keeping this quote in mind, "Change is the only constant phenomenon". Yes, change is what you should always plan with. Even talking about QnAMaker, when I started with writing this book, QnAMaker was in preview and had a very different architecture all together than what it's now built upon. But you should not look at this change as a burden.

© Kasam Shaikh 2019
K. Shaikh, *Developing Bots with QnA Maker Service*,
https://doi.org/10.1007/978-1-4842-4185-1_7

Updating the Knowledgebase

It is not always possible to build an accurate knowledgebase from the end user's perspective. The user, customer, or bot user can make any query, and your FAQ Bot should be ready to deal with it. If not instantly, eventually.

As I detailed in earlier chapters, the QnAMaker service extracts a question and answers it from a given public URL with structured contents, at the time of creating the knowledgebase. It is not always in sync with the URL provided. Consider that at the time of creating the knowledgebase, the URL had eight questions, and later we added eight more questions to the URL content. The eight new questions would not be part of the knowledgebase automatically. You have to explicitly add those new questions to the knowledgebase.

Edit Settings

As stated, there could be a scenario where the URL you added as the source of your FAQ bot was updated at a later point of time. Or consider that you created a bot with a product FAQ, and then later, a new set of questions were added to the product FAQ list. To enable your bot to answer these new questions, you need to update your knowledgebase. To do so, QnAMaker Portal presents you with options through the Edit Settings section.

1. Open the QnAMaker Web Portal and click the My Knowledgebases link on the top menu bar. This page lists all the knowledgebase you created, as shown in Figure 7-1.

2. Click on the name of the knowledgebase you want to edit.

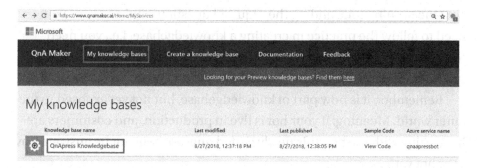

Figure 7-1. *The QnAMaker Web Portal lists the existing knowledgebase services*

You will then see the knowledgebase settings. Here, all the questions and answers associated with your knowledgebase will be listed.

Adding Questions and Answers Manually

There could be scenarios where you have to manually add questions and answers to your knowledgebase, for instance, consider greeting messages. You can add a new question and answer manually using this screen.

Note the +Add QnA Pair text link in Figure 7-2. Click on that link to add a new row in the list of your existing question and answers. Under the Question column, add the text you think the customer or end user will type as the question, and under the Answer column, add the response you want your bot to provide.

Here I will manually add the question, "When will this book be available online?" and answer as, "This book should be available for pre-orders by October 2018."

Note   This is just an example and not the exact dates.

Once you're done adding the required questions and answers, you need to follow the practice in creating a knowledgebase, i.e., you need to Save and Train the changes. Click on Save and Train to add the new questions and answers to the knowledgebase.

Remember, it is now part of knowledgebase, but not yet exposed to the outer world. Meaning, if your bot is live in production, and customers are interacting with the bot, this newly added question will not be answered by your bot yet.

To expose your modified knowledgebase to your live users, you need to follow another practice. Yes! You guessed right, you need to click Publish.

Every time you make a modification to your knowledgebase, you need use Save and Train to save the modification and train the model and then use Publish to make it live!

Figure 7-2. *Link available in QnAMaker Web Portal for adding QnA pairs manually*

Adding Alternate Questions

Queries can be framed in many different ways. It's not always possible to know exactly how your users will frame a question. Again, to make your bot smarter, you need to train your knowledgebase with all possible formations of requests that the users could ask.

Let's consider the question we added. The same question can be asked in several different ways:

- Will the book be available online?

- Can I have the online link for the book, please?

- Is it available only offline?

- What is the date for online availability?

And so on. There could be any number of ways to ask these questions. It all depends on how your bot end user is making the request. We can very well have this in the chat logs captured in Application Insights associated with the QnAMaker service. We will discuss these logs in a later part of this chapter.

You can add alternate questions to your knowledgebase. You can do this on the same edit page. In the grid, under the Question column, in every given row, after every listed question, QnAMaker shows a + icon.

Click the plus icon, and it will present you with a textbox to enter an alternate question. Here you can add different forms of questions, and for all questions, the answer will remain the same as listed under answer column, as shown in Figure 7-3.

I will add the questions mentioned previously to the newly added question earlier in this chapter. Once we add these options, we have to Save and Train to save the knowledgebase and train the model and Publish to make it live.

Now the best part is, while writing this chapter, I noticed a new small but important change being rolled out by the QnAMaker product team. It often happens that we add or modify our knowledgebase but forget to click on Save and Train.

In Figure 7-3, at the top menu bar, notice the Edited* text shown there. This text disappears once you click on Save and Train. This will help QnAMaker users remember to save and train their updated changes.

Knowledge base

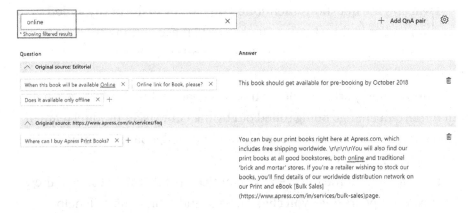

Figure 7-3. *Provision to add alternate questions along with highlighted Edited notification on the top menu bar*

I will verify all these modifications in a later part of this chapter, when I discuss testing the knowledgebase.

The Edit page also has a search functionality. You can search for any word or phrase from within your knowledgebase using this functionality. It shows a textbox at the top of the screen. You just need to add a word and press Enter. I will search for the word "Online," as we just added a question containing this word. See Figure 7-4.

Knowledge base

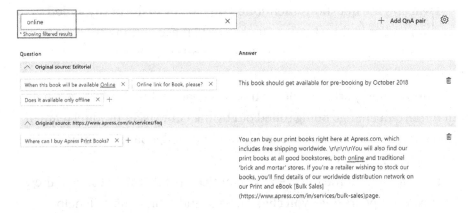

Figure 7-4. *Implementation of the Search functionality in the QnAMaker Web Portal*

This search feature helps in managing a large knowledgebase. You can search for any word and make the changes as required, then click on Save and Train, and you are done. You can efficiently manage a huge knowledgebase with ease.

Adding Filters

Filters in the QnAMaker knowledgebase can be used to narrow your search results, boost answers, and store context. Filters are created as name-value pairs.

At the top-left corner of grid, you will find a setting like icon. Click the icon. It will present you with the third column in the grid, called Filters. You can provide multiple filters for each question listed in the grid.

Again, I will use the same question added to the knowledgebase earlier in this chapter. I am adding the filter with the pair as, `query:Online`, which you can see in Figure 7-5.

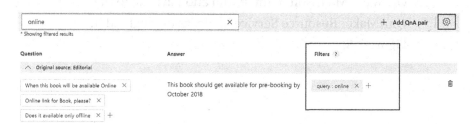

Figure 7-5. *Filters in the QnAMaker Web Portal*

This is just the same as if a user posted a query, and the online QnAMaker knowledgebase will list all answers filtered with the text "online," along with a score of confidence.

Adding Multiple Users to a Knowledgebase

It is always a good idea to have multiple users associated with your knowledgebase. When you deal with huge knowledgebase with multiple documents as input sources, it would be very difficult for a single person to manage it all.

It's smart to add team members responsible for certain input sources as co-users in managing the knowledgebase. The Azure Role-Based Access Control enables multiple people to collaborate on a single knowledgebase.

Note   It would be smart for you to learn about role-based access control and understand what it is at this point in the discussion.

In this section, you'll see how to add a user to the knowledgebase. To do so, follow these steps. This can be achieved using the Azure Portal.

1. Open the Microsoft Azure Portal and navigate to the QnAMaker Resource Service blade, as highlighted in Figure 7-6.

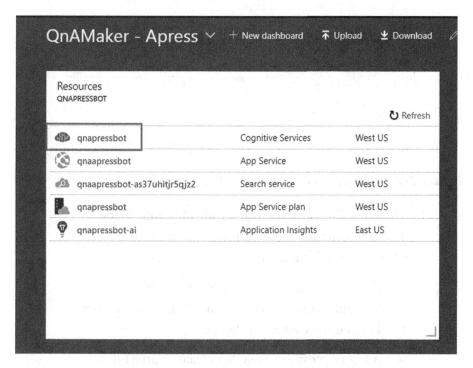

Figure 7-6. Azure Portal Dashboard listing the associated Azure resources

2. From the QnAMaker Resource Service blade, click on the Access Control (IAM) section. You'll then see a window where you can add users with roles. See Figure 7-7.

3. Click the + Add button at the top of the page, as shown in Figure 7-7.

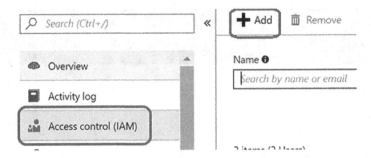

Figure 7-7. *Adding access control in the Azure Portal*

4. Upon clicking Add, you will see an additional blade
    for adding details about permissions (see Figure 7-8).
    Here you need to enter the following details:

    - Role—Provide the role of the newly added user.
      It could be Owner or Contributor. For this chapter,
      I added the user as an Owner.

    - Assign Access to—Specify the access area for the
      new user.

    - Select—Provide the email of the new user.

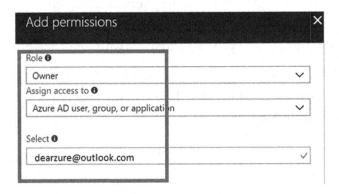

Figure 7-8. *Adding permissions for the new user*

5. Once you're done providing all the details,
    click on Save.

Now when the specified user logs into the QnAMaker Portal, they will be able to access all the knowledgebase services associated with the QnAMaker service.

As you have provided the role to the QnAMaker service, all knowledgebases associated with the service will be accessible to the newly added user.

Note that you cannot provide access to only certain knowledgebases associated with the same QnAMaker service. In such cases, you would have to create multiple QnAMaker services and associate each knowledgebase with all the services. It's like one dedicated QnAMaker service with one knowledgebase. Then you would have to add the user for that specific QnAMaker service only. This way, you can grant access only to specific knowledgebases.

Supported Languages

QnAMaker supports multiple languages for creating knowledgebases. It is recommended that you have one QnAMaker service for each language. For example, if you are planning on having three knowledgebases in three different languages, you should create three QnAMaker services and associate each knowledgebase with the respective QnAMaker.

When you associate a knowledgebase with a QnAMaker service for the first time, the QnAMaker service sets the language of the knowledgebase as the service's language. The service automatically recognize the language from the extracted data and sets the service and knowledgebase language accordingly. You can verify the language of your QnAMaker service from the Azure search resource associated with the QnAMaker service.

Navigate to the Azure Search resource blade and click on the Index file. It will present you with a Fields section. Click on Fields and then check the Analyzer box. This will show the field name rows (Question and Answer in this case) and the associated language under the Analyzer column. Our language is English, as shown in Figure 7-9.

Figure 7-9. *The Azure Search resource blade showing with Fields option with the Analyzer in the Azure Portal*

QnAMaker relies on language analyzers in the Azure search to provide these results. It does support many languages. At the time of writing this book, QnAMaker supports 15+ languages.

During the extraction process, QnAMaker uses keywords to identify questions. Although it supports multiple languages for extraction, the efficiency of extraction is higher for the following languages:

- English

- French

- Italian

- German

- Spanish

To read more about supported languages, visit `http://bit.ly/ qnamakerlanguage`.

The Settings Page of QnAMaker

The best thing about using the QnAMaker service is its easy-to-use user interface. The QnAMaker Web Portal presents you with the Settings page, where you can easily manage your knowledgebase. You can do any of the following:

- Change the knowledgebase service name

  As mentioned earlier in the chapter, the knowledgebase service name we provide while creating the knowledgebase is for referencing purpose and can be changed later. Refer to Figure 7-10.

Figure 7-10. *Changing the knowledgebase service name in the QnAMaker Portal*

- Add/Refresh/Delete documents or URLs added as an input source

  As seen in Figure 7-11, you can add new URLs or documents to add content to your existing knowledgebase. You can also delete URLs or documents.

If you select Refresh Content, the QnAMaker
service will again crawl and extract the contents
from given URLs. As it's a one-time activity and not
always in sync, it's advisable to refresh the content
periodically.

Manage knowledge base

URL	Refresh content	
https://www.apress.com/in/services/faq	☐	🗑
http://		

+ Add URL

File name	
qnapress-doc.docx	🗑
Editorial	🗑

+ Add file

Figure 7-11. *Managing the knowledgebase input source in the QnAMaker portal*

- Export/import a knowledgebase

  If you want to back up your knowledgebase before
  making any changes, or you want to move your
  knowledgebase content to another service, you can
  use the Export Knowledgebase option. Clicking on
  Export Knowledgebase will present you with the
  knowledgebase content in the .tsv (tab separated)
  format. Refer to Figure 7-12.

  You can create a new blank knowledgebase, and
  from the Settings page, import knowledgebases that
  you exported. You can do this by clicking the Import
  Knowledgebase button. It will open a file window,
  allowing you to select the files.

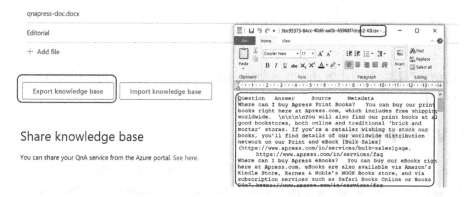

Figure 7-12. Exporting a knowledgebase in the QnAMaker Web Portal

---

Note   When you import a new knowledgebase, it replaces all the existing content from the knowledgebase with content from the imported file. Hence, it's advisable to create a blank knowledgebase before importing.

At the time of writing this chapter, migrating a QnAMaker knowledgebase in preview to a QnAMaker knowledgebase as generally available is achieved by using this Export/Import feature.

- Show a sample HTTP request

    You can display a sample HTTP post request. From the My Knowledge Base page, you click on the View Code option to display the HTTP post request.

- Delete a knowledgebase

    You can delete your knowledgebases from the Settings page. Click the Delete Knowledgebase button, shown in Figure 7-13. A confirmation box will appear. Confirming will delete the knowledgebase.

> Delete knowledge base

Figure 7-13. *You can delete a knowledgebase from the QnAMaker Portal*

Live Chat Logs

The most important logs associated with your FAQ Bot are *chat logs*. Using these logs, you can identify the behavior of your customers with bots in production. The logs tell you the request-response messages that took place with your bot in production.

Using these logs, you can update your knowledgebase, add alternate questions, add filters, add new questions, and more. This helps keep your knowledgebase updated as per customer demands.

In earlier chapters when you created the QnAMaker service, I recommended that you have Application Insights enabled, as all chat logs are saved in Application Insights.

Open the Azure Portal and navigate to the Application Insights resource blade. It's shown in Figure 7-14.

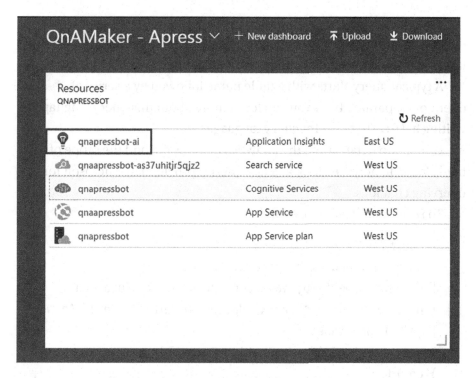

Figure 7-14. *The Azure Portal dashboard lists the associated Azure resources, where Application Insights is highlighted*

Click on the Analytics option presented under the Overview section of the service page, as shown in Figure 7-15.

Figure 7-15. *Link to open the Analytics window in the Application Insights resource blade in the Azure Portal*

This will present you with a page in the portal for querying analytics data being stored. Using this query, you can find all logs that last 24 hours, last 90 days, and even fall within a given date range.

A typical query starts with a table name followed by a series of operators separated by |. You can learn more about this query language by visiting http://bit.ly/logquerylanguage.

Going into detail about the analytics query is beyond the scope of this book. We will, however, look at a few queries provided by Microsoft for querying chat logs.

To review all the logs, use this:

```
requests
| where url endswith "generateAnswer"
| project timestamp, id, name, resultCode, duration
| parse name with *"/knowledgebases/"KbId"/generateAnswer"
| join kind= inner (
traces | extend id = operation_ParentId
) on id
| extend question = tostring(customDimensions['Question'])
| extend answer = tostring(customDimensions['Answer'])
| project KbId, timestamp, resultCode, duration, question,
  answer
```

Paste this query into the portal page after clicking Analytics and then click on Run. Refer to Figure 7-16.

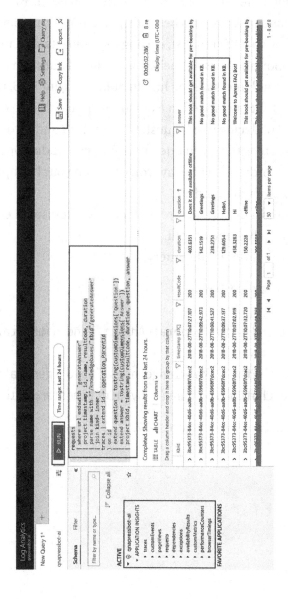

Figure 7-16. Running an analytics query and seeing its output in the Azure Portal

You will be presented with the results with an easy-to-use interface. You can change the time range of the results being fetched. You can also change the timezone of the results being displayed. You can play with the data by filtering any specific request, sorting the requests, and many more.

One of the important parts to analyze is the list of questions that responded with default message. As highlighted in Figure 7-16, there are three such questions that resulted in a default response being sent.

Now you need to decide if this question is relevant and if you think your bot should reply to the given questions. You can update your knowledgebase accordingly. This way, you can keep your bot updated with business and customer demands.

A few more important queries are provided by Microsoft. Let's run each of them and analyze the output.

Total traffic is first. Here is the query:

```
//Total Traffic for 90 Days
    requests
    | where url endswith "generateAnswer" and name startswith
      "POST"
    | parse name with *"/knowledgebases/"KbId"/generateAnswer"
    | summarize ChatCount=count() by bin(timestamp, 1d), KbId
```

The output can be seen in Figure 7-17.

```
//Total Traffic
    requests
    | where url endswith "generateAnswer" and name startswith "POST"
    | parse name with *"/knowledgebases/"KbId"/generateAnswer"
    | summarize ChatCount=count() by bin(timestamp, 1d), KbId
```

Completed. Showing results from the last 24 hours.

timestamp [UTC]	KbId	ChatCount
> 2018-08-27T00:00:00.000	3bc95373-84cc-40d6-aa0b-65968f7dcec2	8

Figure 7-17.   *Query output in the Azure Portal*

You can also query total question traffic in a given time period:

```
//Total Question Traffic in a given time period
    let startDate = todatetime('2018-08-01'); // YYYY-MM-DD
    let endDate = todatetime('2018-08-25');   // YYYT-MM-DD
    requests
    | where timestamp <= endDate and timestamp >=startDate
    | where url endswith "generateAnswer" and name startswith
      "POST"
    | parse name with *"/knowledgebases/"KbId"/generateAnswer"
    | summarize ChatCount=count() by KbId
```

User traffic

```
//User Traffic
    requests
    | where url endswith "generateAnswer"
    | project timestamp, id, name, resultCode, duration
    | parse name with *"/knowledgebases/"KbId"/generateAnswer"
    | join kind= inner (
```

```
traces | extend id = operation_ParentId
) on id
| extend UserId = tostring(customDimensions['UserId'])
| summarize ChatCount=count() by bin(timestamp, 1d),
  UserId, KbId
```

Another important metric is the latency distribution of questions. Latency is the time it takes to complete a single operation. This is the time taken during the request-response of QnA pairs and is a distributed. In Figure 7-18, you can see this distribution based on the time taken for each request. This helps you analyze the performance of your service.

```
//Latency distribution of questions
requests
| where url endswith "generateAnswer" and name startswith
  "POST"
| parse name with *"/knowledgebases/"KbId"/generateAnswer"
| project timestamp, id, name, resultCode, performanceBucket,
  KbId
| summarize count() by performanceBucket, KbId
```

Figure 7-18 shows the output of the latency distribution of questions query.

```
//Latency distribution of questions
requests
| where url endswith "generateAnswer" and name startswith "POST"
| parse name with *"/knowledgebases/"KbId"/generateAnswer"
| project timestamp, id, name, resultCode, performanceBucket, KbId
| summarize count() by performanceBucket, KbId
```

Completed. Showing results from the last 24 hours.

TABLE   CHART   Columns ∨

Drag a column header and drop it here to group by that column

performanceBucket	KbId	count_
> <250ms	3bc95373-84cc-40d6-aa0b-65968f7dcec2	4
> 250ms-500ms	3bc95373-84cc-40d6-aa0b-65968f7dcec2	3
> 500ms-1sec	3bc95373-84cc-40d6-aa0b-65968f7dcec2	1

Figure 7-18. Latency distribution of questions query output in the Azure Portal

Be sure to explore the analytics query language more and play more with the logs being stored in the Application Insights resource associated with your QnAMaker service.

Testing the Knowledgebase

One of the most important phases in any development cycle is the testing phase. It plays an important role in FAQ Bot development. The more accurate your knowledgebase is, the more efficient your FAQ Bot will be for the outer world to talk with.

As you can see in Figure 7-19, the QnAMaker Web Portal presents a smart Testing option to test knowledgebases with a chat window interface. You can experience live talk with your knowledgebase. This not only helps provide a response to a given request, but it also provides all possible answers for a given request with a confidence score. The confidence score measures the accuracy score of a response, with 0 being no confidence and 1 being the highest accuracy/great confidence.

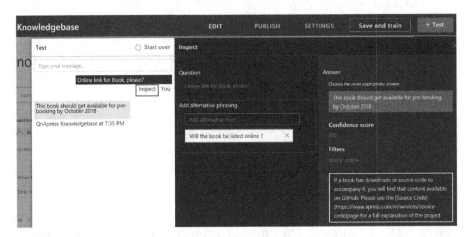

Figure 7-19. *The chat interface for testing your knowledgebase in the QnAMaker Portal*

You can inspect each request and then change the response to the most relevant response listed. Not only this, but you also can provide alternate questions to a given response, straight from the test chat window.

Be sure to Save and Train with every modification you make through the test chat window.

It comes with a clear interface, including a sliding left-right feature. The Test button appears on the top menu bar. Click to open and then again to close.

You must give this smart test feature a try and leverage its capabilities. It will make your knowledgebase and FAQ Bot more efficient for the customers interacting with your bot.

Summary

This chapter discussed the simple but important things you should know about the QnAMaker knowledgebase. It also presented you with the way to manage QnAMaker post-deployment, from updating your knowledgebase content, to analyzing the live chat logs, to adding questions and answers manually. In the coming chapter, you will learn about adding media files, such as image and video files, to your knowledgebase responses. This can make the FAQ Bot smarter and more accurate in terms of responding to user queries.

Happy Learning!

CHAPTER 8

A Step Toward Having an Interactive and Cost-Effective FAQ Bot

In the last chapter, I explained how to manage the QnA Maker knowledgebase, monitor it post deployment, and keep your FAQ Bot updated and ready for incoming customer queries. In this chapter, I will explain how to add media attachments to your QnA Maker-based FAQ Bot response.

Also, as we are on the last chapter of this book, I address a few common myths and queries I am often asked during my sessions. Last but not least, I will mention a few tips and tricks to leverage pricing features of the QnA Maker service at almost no cost!

Adding Hyperlinks

There will be many occasions where you have to redirect your users to different URLs. One of the best ways to do this is to provide links in your responses, such as a hyperlink within the reference text.

© Kasam Shaikh 2019
K. Shaikh, *Developing Bots with QnA Maker Service*,
https://doi.org/10.1007/978-1-4842-4185-1_8

In this case, QnA Maker supports markdown text. QnA Maker extracts the links and converts the HTML to markdown. But it comes with limited conversion capabilities. In this case, you have to manually change the answer text to serve the purpose of hyperlinks. You can update it as follows.

If your text is ABC and you want it to be linked to www.abc.com, you need to update this text in the knowledgebase:

[ABC](www.abc.com)

Reference the text inside square brackets, such as [Text], and add the links using parentheses, such as (Link).

I added a question and answer pair manually, with the answer containing a hyperlink. This is shown in Figure 8-1.

Knowledge base

Figure 8-1. *A QnA pair added with the answer presenting a hyperlink*

You can test the question using the Test panel in the QnA Maker Portal or in the Azure Portal. Choose the Web App Bot ➤ Bot Management ➤ Test in Web Chat section. Figure 8-2 shows the test results.

Figure 8-2. *Chat result in the Test panel*

If you want to attach a file to the response, you can easily present the response with the file download option.

Rich Cards

You cannot add image and video capabilities directly to your QnA Maker knowledgebase.

To accomplish this task, you need to use *rich cards*. For example, you want your FAQ bot to present the users with interactive responses, say an image with a title and a description with a navigation button, or you want a video to play directly in your FAQ Bot response chat window.

At the time of writing this book, the Microsoft Bot Framework supports eight types of rich cards:

- **Adaptive card**—A customizable card containing a combination of text, images, button fields, etc.

- **Animation card**—A card that can play GIFs and short videos.

- **Audio card**—A card that can play audio files.

- **Hero card**—A card that can play images, buttons, and text. I will explain how to use Hero Cards in a later part of this chapter.

- **Thumbnail card**—Similar to a Hero card, but with thumbnail images.

- **Receipt card**—Cards with a receipt structure. Contains a list of items, a total, taxes, etc.

- **SignIn card**—Card to prompt the user to sign in. Contains text with a button to navigate the sign-in process.

- **Video card**—A card for playing videos. I explain this card in a later part of this chapter.

Implementing a Hero Card

Rich cards process events. They come with a `CardAction`, which determines the action that happens when the user interacts with the card. This `CardAction` has the following properties:

- Type—Specifies the type of action to take. This is a `String` property.

- Title—Specifies the title of the button. This is a `String` property.

- Image—Specifies the image URL. This is a `String` property.

- Value—Specifies the values to perform a required type of action. This is a `String` property.

Note   You can read more about rich cards at `http://bit.ly/ botrichcards`.

To implement rich cards, all you have to do is create an object of `CardAction` and set the properties.

Now you might wonder where this code part needs to be added.

1. You have to open the bot code on the IDE. I am using Visual Studio 2017. Open the Microsoft Azure portal and navigate to the Web App Bot Resource blade.

2. Under Bot Management, go to the Build section and download the source code.

3. Open the source code in IDE. Now open the file called `BasicQnAMakerDialog.cs` under the folder named `Dialogs`.

Here you will find the class named `BasicQnAMakerDialog`, which inherits `QnAMakerDialog`.

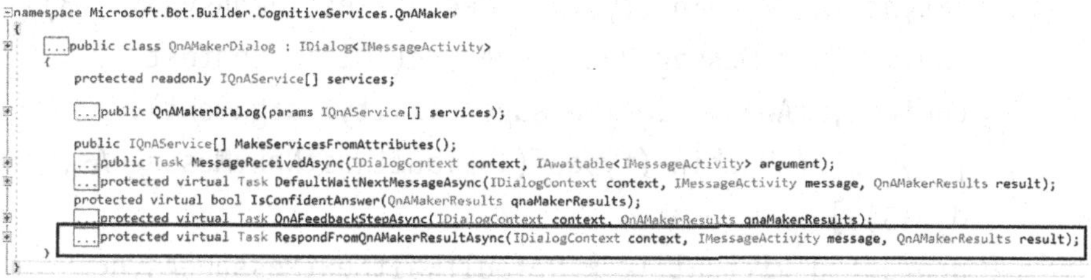

```
namespace Microsoft.Bot.Builder.CognitiveServices.QnAMaker
{
    public class QnAMakerDialog : IDialog<IMessageActivity>
    {
        protected readonly IQnAService[] services;

        public QnAMakerDialog(params IQnAService[] services);

        public IQnAService[] MakeServicesFromAttributes();
        public Task MessageReceivedAsync(IDialogContext context, IAwaitable<IMessageActivity> argument);
        protected virtual Task DefaultWaitNextMessageAsync(IDialogContext context, IMessageActivity message, QnAMakerResults result);
        protected virtual bool IsConfidentAnswer(QnAMakerResults qnaMakerResults);
        protected virtual Task OnAFeedbackStepAsync(IDialogContext context, QnAMakerResults qnaMakerResults);
        protected virtual Task RespondFromQnAMakerResultAsync(IDialogContext context, IMessageActivity message, QnAMakerResults result);
    }
}
```

Figure 8-3. *Code view of the QnA Maker Dialog definition listing its methods*

If you go to the definition of `QnAMakerDialog`, you may notice the method name, `RespondFromQnAMakerResultAsync`. This method sends responses from your QnA Maker. See Figure 8-3.

```
namespace Microsoft.Bot.Builder.CognitiveServices.QnAMaker
{
    //
    // Summary:
    //      A dialog specialized to handle QnA response from
    //      QnA Maker.
    public class QnAMakerDialog : IDialog<IMessageActivity>
    {
        protected readonly IQnAService[] services;

        //
        // Summary:
        //      Construct the QnA Service dialog.
        //
        // Parameters:
        //    services:
        //        The QnA service.
```

```
    public QnAMakerDialog(params IQnAService[] services);

    public IQnAService[] MakeServicesFromAttributes();
    [AsyncStateMachine(typeof(<MessageReceivedAsync>d__8))]
    public Task MessageReceivedAsync(IDialogContext
    context, IAwaitable<IMessageActivity> argument);
    [AsyncStateMachine(typeof(<DefaultWaitNextMessageAsync>
    d__13))]
    protected virtual Task DefaultWaitNextMessageAsync
    (IDialogContext context, IMessageActivity message,
    QnAMakerResults result);
    protected virtual bool IsConfidentAnswer(QnAMakerResul
    ts qnaMakerResults);
    [AsyncStateMachine(typeof(<QnAFeedbackStepAsync>
    d__11))]
    protected virtual Task QnAFeedbackStepAsync(IDialogCont
    ext context, QnAMakerResults qnaMakerResults);
    [AsyncStateMachine(typeof(<RespondFromQnAMakerResultAsy
    nc>d__12))]
    protected virtual Task RespondFromQnAMakerResultAsyn
    c(IDialogContext context, IMessageActivity message,
    QnAMakerResults result);
    }
}
```

In simple words, in order to customize the response, you have to intercept this method. You have to add your code block to this method to implement rich cards, in order to have it in the response.

The only way to use this method is to override what's there, adding the required object initialization of the rich cards. I use a Hero card to add an image as a response from my FAQ Bot.

The Hero card comes with the following properties:

- Title
- Description
- Image URL
- Link to navigate

Before moving to the code part, I will add a QnA pair to the knowledgebase. The answers will be added in the typical way.

Add the values required by the Hero card. The values need to be added with a unique separator. This will allow you to read the response in the code, as shown in Figure 8-4. Now, my answer will appear like this:

```
Title;Description;Link to Navigate; Image URL
```

I add a question and answer using this format and using ; as the separator. This newly added QnA pair can be seen in Figure 8-4.

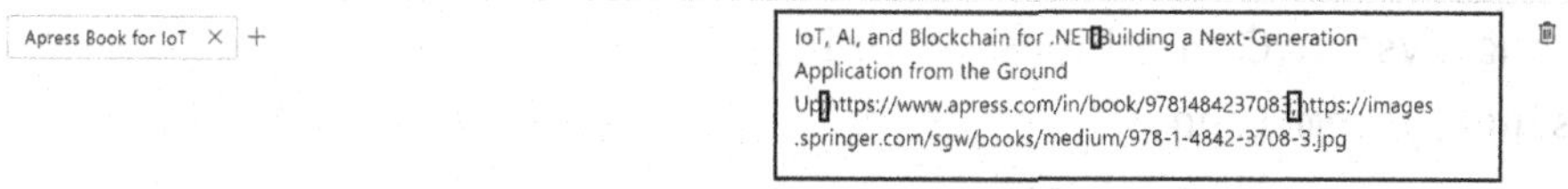

Figure 8-4. *The typical way of writing answers in the QnA pair for a Hero card*

Note   You will get a better understanding of why you have to enter answers using this format when we start writing code.

Once the pair has been added, choose Save and Train and then publish the knowledgebase.

If you test the newly added question, it will respond with a plain text response, as shown in Figure 8-5. This happens because we have not intercepted the response anywhere in the flow.

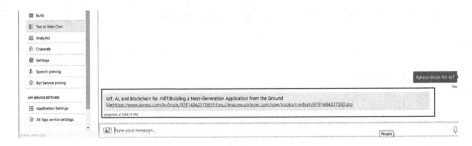

Figure 8-5. *Response received in the Test window in the Azure Portal*

Now let's move to the coding part. I will override the RespondFromQnAMakerResultAsync method and insert the following lines of code:

```
using Microsoft.Bot.Builder.Azure;
using Microsoft.Bot.Builder.CognitiveServices.QnAMaker;
using Microsoft.Bot.Builder.Dialogs;
using Microsoft.Bot.Connector;
using System;
using System.Collections.Generic;
using System.Linq;
using System.Threading;
using System.Threading.Tasks;
protected override async Task RespondFromQnAMakerResultAsync
(IDialogContext context, IMessageActivity message,
QnAMakerResults result)
        {
            var response = result.Answers.First().Answer;

            Activity getInteractiveResponse = ((Activity)
            context.Activity).CreateReply();

            string[] qnaAnswer = reponse.Split(';');
```

```
if (qnaAnswer.Count() > 1)
{
    string title = qnaAnswer[0];
    string description = qnaAnswer[1];
    string url = qnaAnswer[2];
    string imageURL = qnaAnswer[3];

    HeroCard card = new HeroCard
    {
        Title = title,
        Subtitle = description,
    };

    card.Buttons = new List<CardAction>
    {
        new CardAction(ActionTypes.OpenUrl, "Get
        the Book!", value: url)
    };

    card.Images = new List<CardImage>
    {
        new CardImage( url = imageURL)
    };

    getInteractiveResponse.Attachments.Add(card.
    ToAttachment());

    await context.PostAsync(getInteractiveResponse);
}
}
```

I implemented the following changes in this code:

- I overrode the RespondFromQnAMakerResultAsync
  method.

- QnA Maker responds with answer seeded in the
  knowledgebase as a string, which is saved in the
  variable named response.

- As I needed to respond to the user with the
  current bot context, I created an Activity named
  getInteractiveResponse that invokes the CreateReply
  method. It handles replying to the user.

- I added the answer using a unique separator, then I
  read the answer and split it using the same separator.

- Then I created an object of a Hero card and assigned
  the respective values to its properties.

- This card object is now added to
  getInteractiveResponse as an attachment and posted
  back to the user.

Add this code as seen in Figure 8-6 and then build and publish the bot code to the Web App Bot.

Testing the Hero Card

I made this change using an online code editor, which is part of the Bot Management, Build section. Once it is done, I build the bot online. See Figure 8-6.

Figure 8-6. *Code intercepting the response for having an image as the output*

Once the code is deployed, let's test the FAQ Bot response. See Figure 8-7.

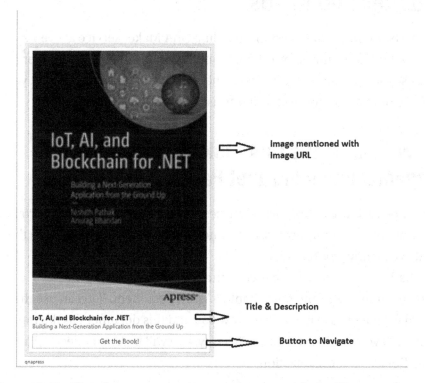

Figure 8-7. *The chat response is set to Image with the Hero card*

167

Great! As you can see in Figure 8-7, with a few lines of code, you can make your FAQ Bot more interactive for your end users.

Note   I used C# as the programming language in these examples. You can also use JSON. The implementation remains the same. Also, for all other cards mentioned in this chapter, you can easily get the code online.

In a very similar fashion, you can add video and other rich cards to your QnA Maker FAQ Bot as responses. The only difference lies in the card properties value.

Queries and Myths

I have been presenting sessions detailing QnA Maker service at events and webinars organized by different online communities. During every QnA session, I am bombarded with the same set of questions. I think you should be aware of these commonly asked questions.

How I Can Make QnA Maker Extract My Organization's Intranet Page?

QnA Maker only extracts publicly accessed URLs. Organizational portals are not open to public access, and hence you cannot directly provide the URL as an input source.

Rather, what you can do is copy the FAQ content from your organization's page and paste it into a Word document. You can use the Word format or save it as a PDF. Now you add this document as the input source to your knowledgebase. This way, you will be able to develop an FAQ Bot for your organization.

Can I Identify Who Is Talking to My FAQ Bot?

No, if you have integrated it into any supported social channels, you cannot. If you are using it on your own website, say using Web Chat embed code, you can ask for user details before displaying the web chat window.

You can also directly develop your chat interface by calling HTTP POST to send a query. While posting a query, along with the parameter question, send the user ID as the second parameter. QnA Maker needs only the first parameter; it has nothing to do with the extra parameters you add to the query string while making a call.

So, the first call would capture the question with user detail, and then second call will be made to the knowledgebase. This way, you can save the chat logs in your database.

Can QnA Maker Extract an Unstructured Format?

At the time of writing this book, it cannot. But the best point is, the QnA Maker product team has set a future roadmap for extracting unstructured data too.

What Is the Max Data Size in Knowledgebase?

It depends on the management pricing tier and the Azure Search pricing tier you select while creating the QnA Maker service.

If you use the free management tier, you will be allowed three managed documents at 1MB each. If you go with the standard tier, there is no limit to the number documents.

There is a trick you should know about when creating your knowledgebase. Using the Azure Portal QnA Maker Resource blade, you can at any point in time change your management pricing tier. Figure 8-8 shows the pricing tier section on the QnA Maker Service Resource blade.

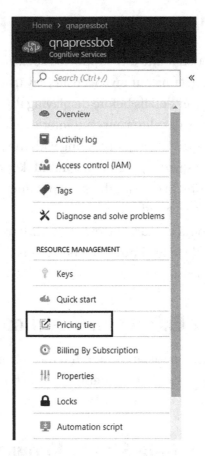

Figure 8-8. *Section allowing you to upgrade the pricing tier in the QnA Maker Resource blade*

Tip   If you want to create a knowledgebase with more than three documents, but using the Free tier, use the steps outlined next.

---

1.   First select the standard QnA Maker Management Pricing Tier.

2.   Go to the QnA Maker Portal and create a knowledgebase associating with this QnA Maker service.

3. Add multiple URLs and documents as source, as required (more than three).

4. Save and Train the knowledgebase.

5. Go back to the Azure Portal, QnA Maker Resource blade.

6. Select the free management pricing tier and click Select to apply it.

Connect and start using the QnA Maker knowledgebase with multiple documents, but still using the free management tier. Here you will be charged only for the time you selected the tier as the standard, on a pro-data basis. That comes to a very negligible amount.

There is no check over the product use, with respect to the management pricing tier. The only check is when you click on Save and Train. When you are saving and training the knowledgebase, it validates the management pricing tier of the QnA Maker service associated with your knowledgebase.

And yes, you can make the most out of this trick, as this product behavior is not termed as an error by the product team.

The last and the best question I have ever come across is the following one.

Does the FAQ Bot Update Its Knowledgebase Automatically as Questions and Queries Come In?

No, it doesn't. It just saves the chat as logs, and you are supposed to feed in the knowledgebase with the updated content.

171

Summary

This book started by introducing you to cognitive services and explaining the Azure cognitive offerings. I explained the real need of QnA Maker and why it is the best choice to go with. I created the service from scratch and then created the backend or brain of the FAQ Bot, the knowledgebase. I explained how to develop and change your bot code, both offline and online.

I introduced you to Azure Bot services, including its offerings and how you can double the intelligence of your FAQ Bot by integrating the QnA Maker knowledgebase and Azure Bot. I connected the FAQ Bot to different social channels, including the Telegram app. I also explained things you should know about regarding your knowledgebase, activities you should perform on your knowledgebase, and post-production deployment. Also, I explained how you can make your FAQ Bot interactive by providing images and explanatory links as responses.

Lastly, I answered some common questions asked about the QnA Maker service and provided a cost-effective approach to building, developing, and using the QnA Maker FAQ Bot.

Before you close the book, I would like to thank you for having the patience to read all the chapters. It's hard to digest 100+ pages for development. But the knowledge I tried sharing here will definitely help you develop a bug-free Bot in minutes.

Again, very best luck to your own FAQ Bot. I would like to hear from you, especially about your experiences and challenges you came across during your FAQ Bot development. And how this book helped you in overcoming the same.

I lead the az-INDIA community for learning Azure. I also organize free webinars for learning Azure, managed by Dear Azure, my baby. I invite you to get connected to this online community.

For sure, you can reach out to me with any queries and concerns during your FAQ Bot development process. You can reach me by email at Kasam@kasamshaikh.com and at Twitter, Facebook, and LinkedIn @KasamShaikh.

Awaiting for your feedback.

Happy Learning!

Index

© Kasam Shaikh 2019
K. Shaikh, *Developing Bots with QnA Maker Service*,
https://doi.org/10.1007/978-1-4842-4185-1

Printed in the United States
by Bookmasters

Printed in the United States
By Bookmasters